The
GREAT
CENTRAL
From the Footplate

Previous page:
The London Midland Region replaced the expresses with semi-fasts. The 08.15 Nottingham-Marylebone is seen leaving Aylesbury with 'Britannia' Pacific No 70014 *Iron Duke* in charge in March 1961. *G. C. Farnell*

Below:
There are only three days to go on the last semi-fast services as 'Black Five' No 45493 prepares to leave Marylebone with the 14.38 to Nottingham Victoria on 1 September 1966. Driver Wallace Needle looks back down the platform. *J. H. Bird*

The GREAT CENTRAL

From the Footplate

LONDON

IAN ALLAN LTD

Robert Robotham and Frank Stratford

Dedication:
This book is dedicated to the memory of Bill Strong of Marylebone Diesel Depot, who was tragically killed in a shunting accident at Wendover.

Acknowledgements
Special thanks are due to M. A. Robotham, G. C. Farnell, J. E. Green, R. Clemons, B. O. Hilton and H. Gamble.

First published 1988

ISBN 0 7110 1759 X

Published by Ian Allan Ltd, Shepperton, Surrey; and printed by Ian Allan Printing Ltd at their works at Coombelands in Runnymede, England

Contents

Preface

Every railway in Britain has its own unique character. That character comes mostly from the circumstances in which the line was built and started operating and also from the people who ran it. The Great Central (GC) main line was no exception to this. GC operating methods differed drastically from those of other lines around it, having originated from the GC's desire and need to compete with its arch rival the Midland Railway, and continued through LNER ownership right through to the closure of the line by BR in 1966. Many GC men could never really accept that the London Midland Region (LMR) was in charge after February 1958, but they soon saw the results of the transfer in terms of rationalisation and run-down as East Midland services were concentrated on the Midland Line to St Pancras. The GC also attracted a fierce loyalty of patronage from its customers, with trains such as the 'Master Cutler', and gave Nottingham and Leicester an excellent service not only on the routes from London-Sheffield and Manchester, but also on the cross-country lines. The closure of the GC took away most of these services and whilst London services on the Midland now have InterCity 125 trains, passengers now have to change at Derby, Birmingham and Nuneaton for cross-country destinations. Goods and parcel services, like the passenger trains, were usually run at high speeds — the superb line formation and alignments requiring few speed restrictions until the process of run-down began.

There is no doubt that the GC spirit produced what must have been some of the finest locomotive crews that this country has ever seen. Perhaps it is not surprising that 'Top Shed', Haymarket and Old Oak Common have always had more press, but certainly the success of the postwar GC's services was due to the dedication of the staff at its depots at Neasden, Annesley and Leicester Central. Annesley provided crews for a variety of jobs, but mainly for the famous Annesley to Woodford fast freights, the modified Class Fs, that usually travelled at speeds in excess of 50mph and were arguably the most efficiently operated freight services in Britain. Leicester and Neasden provided the crews for the majority of the expresses (their forefathers had run the 'Sheffield Special' from Marylebone to Sheffield in only 2hr 50min in 1914, InterCity 125s in 1986 on the Midland Line manage St Pancras-Sheffield in 2hr 22min!) and their spirit had continued through to and even after the withdrawal of the expresses. These men really were good and knew exactly how to get the best out of their engines — indeed they had to, if they were to achieve some of the timings that existed on the section between Nottingham, Leicester and Aylesbury.

Frank Stratford is a man who embodies this unique spirit and it is, in my opinion, a tragedy that people of his calibre have been lost to our railway industry. He has been a railway enthusiast for as long as he can remember and started work as an engine cleaner at Leicester Central shed on 7 January 1952. With the run-down of the GC main line and the inevitable loss of work at Leicester, he was made redundant in December 1963, but by February 1964 he had transferred to Marylebone where he spent a happy two years until he transferred, on the GC's closure, to Leicester Midland where he left in April 1969 under a redundancy arrangement.

I hope that this book, which is intended to complement *The Last Years of the Great Central Main Line*, will show just how unique the GC spirit was. It is offered as a tribute to all those who made the line one of Britain's truly great railways.

Robert Robotham
Nottingham, 1987

**Fairburn '4MT' 2-6-4T
No 42250 waiting for the
'off' with an Aylesbury
service in October 1961,
has a good head of steam
on for the fast climb
through the Chilterns.
Marylebone looks very
much the same in 1987.**
G. C. Farnell

Postwar Traffic on the Great Central

Robert Robotham

Express and local passenger services

The postwar GC express service consisted of six expresses up to London and seven returning north in the down direction, all the daytime trains being restaurant car expresses. The business market was won back after the war with excellent trains such as the 'Master Cutler', which left Sheffield for London at 07.40, calling at Nottingham, Leicester and Rugby. The return service left Marylebone at 18.18. Timings were smart, but due to wartime neglect, were not initially as fast as the original Great Central expresses, although there was gradual improvement. The other named service was the 'South Yorkshireman', which left Bradford for Marylebone at 10.00, the down working leaving London at 16.50. The reliability and fast running of these expresses was mostly due to the brilliance of the GC footplate crews. Speed restrictions north of Nottingham and tight pathing between suburban services south of Aylesbury and the GW expresses on the joint line through High Wycombe, resulted in a requirement for very fast running between Aylesbury and Nottingham.

Motive power for these expresses was normally provided by 'A3s', 'V2s' and 'B1s' during the Eastern Region days, but LMS and BR Standard types appeared after February 1958 when the line became part of the London Midland Region. From that date the downgrading of the Main Line began almost immediately. The 'Master Cutler' service was withdrawn from the line and subsequently ran as a Pullman train to Sheffield from King's Cross via Retford. By January 1960 GC line expresses had been replaced by a semi-fast service that ran between Nottingham and Marylebone only. Fast trains from London to the Midlands were concentrated

'V2' 2-6-2 No 60863 tears through Princes Risborough with a Boys' Brigade special for an anniversary parade in Hyde Park in June 1957. Leicester Fireman Ron Cassie looks out for the next set of signals.
G. C. Farnell

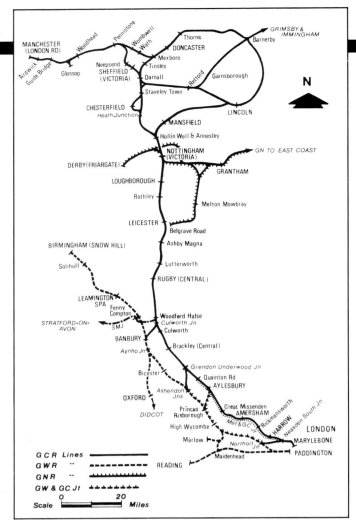

Left:
The Great Central main line and its associated routes.

Cross country workings

The GC main line had been connected to the GWR at Banbury since 1900 on a direct line from Woodford Halse. This allowed long-distance express passenger services from the North to call at the biggest towns in the East Midlands, Leicester and Nottingham, en route to the South-West or South-East of England — a facility that no longer exists today as all cross-country services currently run through Derby. The most famous of these cross-country services was the Bournemouth-York express that continued to run over the line until it was closed, but others ran to all parts of the BR system taking their locomotives and crews with them in many cases. It was usually the case that locomotives were changed at Banbury but some ran through to Oxford and even Swindon on a regular basis. Thus on the GC main line a 'V2' could be followed by a 'Hall' or a 'Grange', which in turn could be followed by an 'A3' and then a 'Black Five'. The GC was truly a locomotive spotter's paradise.

Special traffic

The GC became a very useful diversionary route and from 1951 relieved Euston of parcels trains which travelled up to Bletchley via the junction at Claydon (laid during World War 2) which offered access to the Oxford-Bletchley line. When the West Coast main line was undergoing electrification in the early 1960s, Marylebone took some extra parcels traffic and the Manchester sleepers. The GC's proximity to Wembley Stadium resulted in its use by many specials which ran to Wembley from all parts of Britain. Special workings for Rugby League Cup Finals, Women's Hockey Internationals and FA Cup Finals brought many different locomotive types and it was not uncommon to see 'Royal Scots', 'Halls', 'West Country' Pacifics, 'V2s' and 'B1s' all in the same sidings. The then equivalent of today's 'Nightrider' service, known as the 'Starlight Special', was also operated to Scotland from Marylebone. It was a real bargain at a price of £3.50 return and loaded well. Marylebone also saw Motorail traffic to Glasgow, Perth and Stirling during this period.

The semi-fasts

The withdrawal of the GC expresses in January 1960 heralded a new semi-fast service that ran over the line between Nottingham and Marylebone, with local services continuing. There were three trains in either direction, all loading to six coaches except the 17.15 Nottingham-Marylebone which had seven. No GC line trains were scheduled to run via High Wycombe. There were other long-distance services that conveyed passengers, notably the Marylebone-Manchester mail and its up balancing working, the 03.40 mail and passenger coaches from Marylebone to Nottingham — a very slow service that took 5hr, — and the York to Swindon mails. By March 1963 most of the local services had been withdrawn and the semi-fasts were adjusted slightly to take this into account. There was a reduction to four coaches in all services, except the 17.15 up

on the St Pancras route, the business express to the East Midlands becoming the 'Robin Hood'.

Leicester Central was the focal point of GC express operations — most trains stopping to change crews or locomotives — a process that took only 4min. The fast workings were complemented by a local service that called at the smaller stations. Some services operated as long-distance stoppers — the most famous being the evening local from Sheffield to Leicester and return, locally known as the 'Spitfire', due to its rapid turn-around at Leicester. Renowned also was the ubiquitous 'Banbury Motor', that linked the GC with the Great Western main line at Banbury. These trains were known as 'ords' to staff; others ran between Nottingham and Leicester; between Leicester, Rugby and Woodford; and between Woodford, Aylesbury and Marylebone. Some of these local workings saw Western Region haulage on their southern runs with locomotives that had worked cross-country expresses as far as Leicester from the south and west. The 'ords' were usually worked by 'K3s', 'K2s', 'L1s' and ex-GCR 'Directors'.

Suburban services from Marylebone ran on an intensive basis as far as Aylesbury or Princes Risborough on the GW/GC Joint Line. A few services ran on the branch from Aylesbury to 'Risborough and thence to Maidenhead on the branch from High Wycombe. The latter were usually formed of WR auto-trains whilst motive power for the suburban stoppers was provided by LNER 'L1' 2-6-4Ts and latterly LMS Fairburn 2-6-4Ts before diesel multiple units (DMUs) replaced them.

which kept its seven, the three extra being used to make up the coaching stock for the return Marylebone-Manchester mail. The 08.38 and 12.25 from Marylebone and Nottingham respectively were worked by a four-car DMU. The service was not very attractive to the long-distance traveller — fast trains being concentrated at St Pancras. The semi-fasts were the 08.15, 12.25 and 17.15 from Nottingham, and the 08.38, 14.38 and 16.38 from Marylebone.

Motive power was usually provided by anything that the other regions had dispensed with — ie, worn-out 'Royal Scots', 'Britannias' and usually the LMS 'Black Fives'. 'B1s' and 'V2s' did very occasionally put in an appearance. With steam shed closures abounding, Annesley had become the last GC steam shed to remain open in mid-1965. It thus became Banbury's task to provide the maintenance for the southern end of the line (Cricklewood and Willesden having closed), though this was really of little use if a locomotive failed at Marylebone. There is one horror story of 'Black Five' No 45375 failing at Woodford with the 08.15 from Nottingham, the replacement locomotive itself failing at Banbury and the train eventually arriving at Marylebone 3hr 20min late with No 44843 in charge. With no coaling facilities at Marylebone, locomotives had to run on an 'out-and-home' basis and this requirement resulted in some 'Britannias' with high-capacity tenders being allocated to the line. Even water provision was unreliable, especially if the columns at Brackley and Aylesbury were out of use. Water stops at Great Missenden were not uncommon, the process of filling a tender sometimes taking up to 45min!

Colwick shed assumed responsibility for the supply of motive power in late 1965 on Annesley's closure and the semi-fasts struggled on for nine more months before being replaced by the truncated 'death throes' service of DMUs between Nottingham and Rugby only.

Freight traffic

The GC was not just a passenger carrying line, indeed freight was its most important traffic in terms of both volume and revenue. These services were operated in the same cavalier spirit as the expresses. The main flow was between Annesley and Woodford and consisted mainly of fast goods trains known as 'Windcutters' or 'Runners' due to the high speed at which they travelled. The line was simple to operate, and the 60 miles between Annesley and Woodford saw the coal trains supplemented with steel and general merchandise traffic from the North-East and Yorkshire which ran to the south via Banbury and the Stratford & Midland Junction (S&MJ) line to Honeybourne and Ashchurch. These services were run mostly as express freights with a small number of local trips running for the intermediate stations — the Woodford trip being known to the footplate crews as the 'Round the World'. The main line services were mostly run loose-coupled with short-wheelbase, unbraked wagons. These Annesley-Woodford services ran on an 'out-and-home' basis from the yards and must rank as one of the most efficient services ever operated by British Railways. Annesley provided the motive power — usually a BR '9F' 2-10-0 which was serviced by Woodford shed on arrival. Discipline was high on these trains — it had to be because trains were cancelled if locomotives were late. Limited to 50 wagons, with some 30 workings in each direction each day, these trains were known as Modified Class Fs and frequently ran at speeds of up to 50mph. The '9Fs' replaced the ER 'O1' and 'O4' 2-8-0s — many locomotives working two round trips per day — a distance of 280 miles. Woodford dealt with 44 northern arrivals and 43 departures, plus 47 southern arrivals and 58 departures per day — an astonishing three million wagons passing through each year. Whilst most of the 'Runners' joined the GW line to the South-West and Wales at Banbury, many of the steel trains, known as 'Door Knockers', travelled via the S&MJ to the GW — indeed the line had to be upgraded for this purpose. Ten workings per day carried semi-finished steel from Consett or Scunthorpe to South Wales via Fenny Compton and Honeybourne, the trains usually being headed by WD 'Austerity' 2-8-0s or WR double-chimney '9Fs'. Not as much freight went south on the main line route but there was a daily York Dringhouses-Marylebone express freight and a twice-weekly Class C Guinness train for the Park Royal brewery from Newcastle. Due to the congestion on the Aylesbury and Rickmansworth route, these trains travelled via High Wycombe.

Other notable services were the traditional GC fish trains — again run as expresses. These ran from Grimsby to Whitland and the South-West and from Hull to Plymouth. The 1953 and, to a lesser extent, 1955 ASLEF strikes hit BR's freight traffic hard, the fish trains being no exception. By the early 1960s, they were running with average payloads of only 35½ tons, which did not even cover their running costs. Leicester crews worked these trains which were usually headed by 'K3s' or Immingham 'Britannias'. Other long-distance freights ran on the NE/SW axis in both directions — usually with 'foreign' 'V2s', 'B16s' or 'K3s' in charge.

Cross-country parcels services ran through the GC system, the notable one being the 06.50 Banbury-York known as the 'Rabbits' due to its cargo. Night mails from Swindon to York

and return, as well as the diverted trains from Euston, also ran, as well as the ubiquitous Marylebone-Manchester and return mail. The 'crack' train was the GC newspaper service which left Marylebone at 01.40 and was at Rugby at 03.32 and at Leicester at 04.05.

The last booked freight train ran over the GC on 11 June 1965 and all the aforementioned services were either discontinued for good or transferred to other lines.

Run-down and closure

The rationalisation of BR had started just after Nationalisation in 1948. The railways were no longer seen (at high level at any rate) as competing routes and it soon became clear that two routes to the East Midlands could no longer be retained. The huge losses BR was bound to make could no longer be tolerated either.

The intended fate of the GC did not become clear until the London Midland Region took over the GC from February 1958. All express trains went by January 1960 and the replacement semi-fasts did not offer the most attractive service. The cross-country service was reduced to just one train — the York-Bournemouth. Although initially freight traffic was still very heavy, most of it was eventually either lost for good or diverted. The Annesley-Woodford coal workings were replaced by 'Merry-Go-Round' pit-to-power station block train workings which ran over the Midland line owing to the fact that it wound rather conveniently around the waters of the Trent needed by the new power stations.

By 1963 the local services were withdrawn and all but a few stations were closed. Steam depots were also closed which made maintenance difficult. In some cases, locomotives which failed at the London end of the line could not be remedied as the nearest steam depot was Banbury. Maintenance was slashed and some signalbox closures resulted in block sections nearly 20 miles long. One driver even had to stop his train and climb a signal post to clean a signal lens to see what colour it was. It is indeed a credit to those operating staff that any service continued at all.

The last workings ran on 3 September 1966. The 08.15 Nottingham-Marylebone saw 'Black Five' No 44872 which failed at Aylesbury, being replaced by Class 24 No D5089. The 08.38 from Marylebone and its return working the 12.25 from Nottingham was formed of the usual DMU. Class 24 diesel No D5000 had the 14.38 from Marylebone and 'Black Five' No 45292 the 16.38. As well as these normal service trains, rebuilt 'Merchant Navy' Pacific No 35030 *Elder Dempster Lines* hauled a special from Waterloo to the Nottingham area and thence to Marylebone. The train was composed of green Southern Region stock. 'Black Five' No 45267 headed the 12.40 Rugby-Nottingham local and the York-Bournemouth and return was hauled in both directions by Class 47 diesel No D1572.

The last star performer was 'Black Five' No 44984 from Colwick, which hauled the 17.15 to Marylebone, and then followed with the final 22.45 (SO) Mail, rather fittingly, to Manchester. 'Black Five' No 44858 was in charge of the 00.09 Sheffield-Swindon between Nottingham Victoria and Leicester and the 00.45 Mail from Sheffield to Marylebone between Leicester and Woodford. She then ran to Banbury for disposal. Thus, the last main line services ended in the early hours of 4 September 1966.

Bottom left:
'9F' No 92087 forges up the bank to Staverton Road signalbox on 20 April 1965. The bridge in the foreground spanned the one time Rugby to Leamington branch.
M. Mitchell

Top right:
With snow lying on the lineside '9F' 2-10-0 No 92168 tops Ashby Magna bank with an up 'Windcutter' on 23 January 1965. *M. Mitchell*

Centre right:
'Black Five' 4-6-0 No 44858 heads for Marylebone with the 08.15 from Nottingham Victoria, and is seen south of Moor Park on 24 August 1966.
P. H. Groom

Below:
Thompson 'O1' 2-8-0 No 63630 passes another freight at Nottingham Victoria, whilst in the bay on the right stand locals to Grantham and Basford North (via Gedling) powered by 'J39' 0-6-0 No 64832 ND 'J6' 64230 respectively. January 1958. *J. Cupit*

Top left:
**An early hours shot of '9F'
No 92183 at Nottingham
on the 20.45 Marylebone-
Doncaster parcels on
19 December 1965.**
J. Clarke

Bottom left:
**A typical GC Annesley-
Woodford 'Runner', with
'9F' No 92072 in charge,
storms through Rugby
en route for Woodford on
2 January 1965.**
Ian Allan Library

Right:
**'Royal Scot' 4-6-0
No 46126** *Royal Army
Service Corps* **heads past
Leicester Goods South
with the 10.10
Nottingham-Neasden
empty vans on 13 April
1963.** *G. D. King*

Below:
**Leicester 'A3' Pacific
No 60102** *Sir Frederick
Banbury* **passes the same
spot in charge of the 08.25
Manchester-Marylebone
on 23 March 1957.**
B. O. Hilton

2

Leicester Central Shed

Frank Stratford

Humble beginnings

To start a traction career on British Railways, one had to begin at the very bottom as an engine cleaner. There was no way to leapfrog to the top, even if one's father was the shed master. The railway worked strictly on seniority and, whereas an apprentice in a trade such as carpentry or building could have qualifications after five years, one had to be prepared for a much longer road to the top of the tree in the footplateman's trade.

At Leicester Central shed, as well as cleaning engines, we were also utilised on such duties as drying and riddling the sand in the sandhouse, emptying the ash pits, and stints up 'hungry hill' (the coal stage). This job entailed shovelling coal from wagons into the small tubs which were then pushed out and emptied into the locomotive tenders. When there were a lot of engines to be coaled this could be a very strenuous job indeed. The minimum age to be passed for firing duties was 16, so in my case I had almost a year on the above mentioned duties.

The link structure

Leicester Central was only a small depot, but the work was very good, consisting mostly of passenger turns, a good many of which were mileage turns to London, Manchester (until the electrification over the Pennine route was completed) and Swindon. The bottom link was the shed and pilot link; No 3 link, the first main line link encountered, covered local passenger freight and pick-up workings. No 2 mainly covered express passenger services and also worked all special traffic.

The top link, No 1, encompassed all the top expresses including the 'Master Cutler' and the 'South Yorkshireman'.

Day-to-day life at Leicester Central

Life at Leicester Central on a day-to-day basis was very varied and interesting, especially after one had been passed for firing duties. As a passed cleaner one had to go on shift work. The shifts at Leicester were 04.00 and 08.00 on days and 14.00 and 21.00 on nights and afternoons. (The reasons for these times was to coincide with the jobs at the depot, as if firemen failed to turn up for duty, then the passed cleaners would be used as firemen.)

An interesting point worth noting here is the fact that at the time I became a passed cleaner at 16 years of age, I was immediately put on the above mentioned shifts as was everyone else. It wasn't until the Midland shed took over the administration of Leicester Central that we discovered that men under 18 couldn't work officially on night shifts and a number of lads had to be hurriedly placed back on days! Apparently, the law had been relaxed during World War 2 and the depot had just carried on since then.

The rostering at Leicester consisted of three main line links, each with 12 sets of men, together with a shed and pilot link, also with 12 sets of men. At most depots it was common to have a spare link to work specials and cover for men on holiday or off sick, but at Leicester Central a system of link-to-link promotion operated. This meant that should a man be off in the top link, the man on the nearest turn to him in No 2 link would move up to his job, the nearest man in No 3 would move up to cover the vacancy in No 2 link, and a passed cleaner would get a firing job.

If a man was off for a week or more, it would not be the nearest man in the link below who took his turn of duty, but

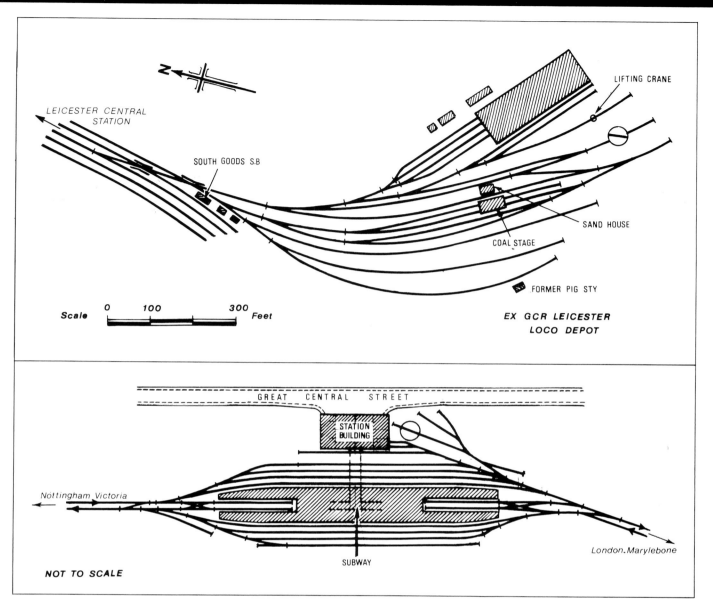

Scale 0 100 300 Feet

EX GCR LEICESTER
LOCO DEPOT

LEICESTER CENTRAL
STATION

SOUTH GOODS S.B

LIFTING CRANE

SAND HOUSE

COAL STAGE

FORMER PIG STY

GREAT CENTRAL STREET

STATION BUILDING

Nottingham Victoria

London.Marylebone

SUBWAY

NOT TO SCALE

the senior hand on the same shift in the link below. This promotion could sometimes make one worse off. For example, when I was firing in No 2 link, one of our best jobs was taking the 16.42 to Marylebone and returning with the Doncaster parcels. This was a 'mileage' turn, paying 6hr extra for the number of miles worked. The nearest turn to this in No 1 link was working the 15.20 Marylebone-Sheffield and returning with the London mail. This was not a mileage turn and I was often moved up on to this job for odd days, thereby losing 6hr pay! On this theme, I well remember one particular driver who used to find out from the holiday roster what job his holidays would fall on and, if it happened to be a good mileage turn, he would immediately swop his holidays, so he only missed a flat week.

As a passed cleaner it was essential to get as many firing turns as possible as, for every 250 turns worked, a rise in pay was forthcoming. On the 04.00 cleaning shift, it was unusual for a week to go by without one of the early turn firemen 'having a daft one', so we used to get a pretty regular diet of firing duties.

Top:
Track plan of Leicester Central Motive Power Depot as at 1953.

Above:
Track plan of Leicester Central station as at 1963.

Leicester's characters

Like any other depot, I suppose, Leicester Central had its share of real characters. When I first began my career, there were still a few drivers around who had started in the pre-Grouping era and one or two of them were stern taskmasters who used to strike awe into a young cleaner. When George Crewe was on the 'Master Cutler', we had to ask his permission to board his engine, just to clean the footplate and cab windows.

There was a driver known as 'Rubber' as his name was Tom Eales. There was the 'Pig Man' Jack Jacques — so called as he and his father, also a driver, raised pigs in a sty at the side of the shed. A driver in the shed link named Fred Thrall was up to all sorts of tricks, and you had to be on your guard not to get caught. I well remember him once horribly catching out a certain fireman. The said fireman had a habit of poking the mess room fire out whenever he arrived on duty. This used to cause dust and a smell that annoyed Fred if he was on his meal break. On the day in question, knowing what time the man was on duty, he preheated the handle end of the poker in the fire. It had just lost its red glow when in walked the fireman who, true to form, went to perform his poking duties. Needless to say, he dropped the poker rather more quickly than he picked it up!

There were other characters such as Norman Ward who was known as the 'Baron' as he owned a smallholding. A passed fireman, whose name I won't mention, was known as 'Burglar Bill' because he had to have a close look at anything that wasn't screwed down. There was a Sid 'Kamakaze' Cooper and 'Regulator' Robson, who could both 'knock them along a bit'. Some of the nicknames fitted very well, but I never did know the origins of others, such as 'Tanky' Joe Burgess, whose father was a King's Cross driver who had handled an 'A4' during the 1948 locomotive exchanges, and Albert 'Chuff Chuff' Chafer who called everybody 'Henry lad'. My old mate Ron Smith who was known as 'Radar Ron', Les Bilson, known as the 'Bishop', 'Horrible Horace', and many others. A well known cockney at the depot was Arthur Dodd, who was a good mate when things were going well, but on a bad 'Black Five' it was an education to see him hopping around from one side of the cab to the other shouting that everything LMS should be 'dumped in the ocean'. He could always be heard in the mess room

recounting a tale of woe and became known as 'everything happens to Arthur'.

Another nickname bestowed upon Ted Rodwell, although rather unkind, showed the wit that abounded at the depot. After missing the distant signal at Lutterworth one day (see p64) and colliding with a freight train, he was named 'Mister Magoo' after a well known short-sighted cartoon character of the time. One could go on forever about the various characters encountered, but one I must mention was top link Driver Ernie Warren. Ernie was a superb engineman, who was proud of his 'middle gear' driving, and scoffed at anyone who 'thrashed' an engine. He was always ready with a quick retort and told me many tales that brought a smile. One such story concerned him working up to Marylebone with Neasden 'A3' No 60111 *Enterprise* which they were leaving in London, and bringing a Leicester engine back. No 60111 was due for overhaul and in a poor condition for an 'A3'. The engine was very heavy on water and they had a job to keep time. Ernie was telling the Neasden foreman Harold Floyd about it to which Harold replied that he thought the piston rings had gone. 'Gone' replied Ernie, 'I'll say they're gone, they're in a bloody field at Grendon!'

Ernie was also heard to remark at Woodford shed one day, on seeing a GWR '28xx' 2-8-0, 'Some engine that — it's got two broomsticks holding the smokebox up'. However, Ernie himself was left speechless one day when comparing notes with a Darnall man about 'B1' No 61090. Ernie had worked the engine the day previously and thought what a good 'B1' it was. The 'grinder' complained that his mate couldn't maintain the water level in the boiler when working up Staveley Bank. When asked by Ernie how he worked the engine he replied 'Reet across and a turn and a half up the rack'. To the uninitiated, this meant full regulator and roughly 50% cut-off! No wonder 'middle gear' Ernie was speechless. Just in passing, another amusing nickname comes

The 08.25 to London is seen again on 2 August 1958 with 'V2' No 60878 in charge *G. D. King*

to mind. An old goods guard at Leicester, Bill Golightly, was known affectionately by a lot of the drivers as 'Tread Heavy'!

Two other passenger guards who liked a drop were Bill Skins, who was known to dash up the stairs to the pub during a 10min stop at Chesterfield, and Guard Bramley who rejoiced under the nick-name of 'cockerel neck'.

Motive power

The motive power on the GC line was always interesting and during my service changed considerably over the years. When I first started, the 'A3' Pacifics were on all the top jobs, with the ubiquitous 'B1' 4-6-0s on most of the other passenger work. The 'Footballer' 4-6-0 'B17s' had by then left Leicester and only one or two remained at Colwick. The 'A3s' were later to be swapped for 'V2' 2-6-2s and the 'B1s' also had to share their duties with LMS 'Black Five' 4-6-0s and BR Standard types. Various 0-6-0s were shedded at Leicester over the years, including examples of Classes J2, J5, J6, J11 and J39. 'J52' No 68839, the long-standing goods pilot, was eventually replaced by LMS '3F' 0-6-0T No 47203.

Also encountered by Leicester men were Woodford 'K3' 2-6-0s, WD 'Austerity' 2-8-0s, 'O4' 2-8-0s from Darnall which used to work to Leicester, the occasional 'O2' and various oddments such as 'B16s', and Annesley 'O1s'. The class leader of the GC 'A5' 4-6-2Ts, No 69800, was also at Leicester for a number of years.

Leicester Central was an Eastern Region shed until the London Midland Region took over in 1958. Until then the shed code was 38C, but under the LMR it was 15E from 1958 to 1963 and 15D from 1963 until it closed in July 1964, after which its locomotives were reallocated to Annesley (16B). Leicester Belgrave Road was a sub-shed on the GNR line. It closed in June 1955. The engines came from Colwick (38A) from 1950 but Leicester provided the crews.

LOCOMOTIVE ALLOCATIONS – LEICESTER CENTRAL MPD

Date: 1955-56
Region: Eastern
Shed Code: 38C

60049	*Galtee More*	60820	61369
60052	*Prince Palatine*	60863	61380
60054	*Prince of Wales*	60878	61381
60059	*Tracery*	61088	64375
60102	*Sir Frederick Banbury*	61141	64438
60104	*Solario*	61185	68839
60107	*Royal Lancer*	61298	
60111	*Enterprise*	61299	

Date: Summer 1959
Region: London Midland
Shed Code: 15E

40165	60831	61008	*Kudu*	61137	61376
40182	60842	61028	*Umseke*	61201	61380
47203	60863	61063		61269	61381
	60879	61085		61298	64256
	60911	61106		61369	

Date: January 1963
Region: London Midland
Shed Code: 15E

42437	44830	45238	73156
42453	44847	45277	
42556	44848	45335	
	44984	45342	
	45223	73069	

Right:
Leicester Central shed on 16 July 1962. 'K3' 2-6-0 No 61883 has its pony truck removed for attention whilst 'V2' No 60890 has sadly been put into store.
H. A. Gamble

Below right:
Bay Platforms 3 and 4 at Leicester Central station on 15 December 1955. 'B1' 4-6-0 No 61188 is waiting to take on the up 'South Yorkshireman', while King's Cross 'A3' No 60062 *Minoru* has been borrowed by Neasden shed and will return home on the 14.04 to Marylebone. The three men on the platform are Driver George Kendall, Inspector Percy Banyard and Shunter Jim Toone. *P. H. Wells*

Left:
The engine on which Frank Stratford spent many happy hours as a young passed cleaner — Leicester's 'J52' 0-6-0T No 68839, pictured at rest outside the shunters' cabin on 23 April 1957. The tall structure in the background is Leicester City Football Club's Filbert Street ground. *B. O. Hilton*

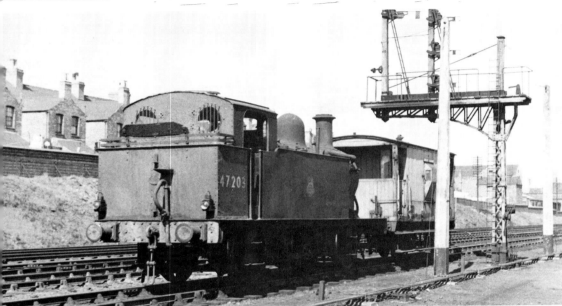

Below left:
'Jinty' 0-6-0T No 47203 replaced No 68839 as Leicester's shunter. It is seen at Leicester South Goods on 12 March 1958. *B. O. Hilton*

Bottom:
'B1' No 61182 storms through Bulwell Common with the 10.00 ex-Marylebone to Manchester on 22 March 1952. *J. F. Henton*

Above:
Unusual power for the petrol sidings shunt from Abbey Lane sidings is provided by 'Royal Scot' No 46122 *Royal Ulster Rifleman* on 6 October 1964. The empty tanks are about to be backed into the sidings at Leicester Goods South.
Ian Allan Library

Left:
'A3' Pacific No 60052 *Prince Palatine* leaves Leicester Central with the up 'South Yorkshireman' on 6 August 1955.
J. F. Henton

Top right:
By 1963, London Midland Region locomotives were dominating GC services, along with BR types. Eastern Region locomotives were not common and it was left to 'Black Five' No 44821 to take the 13.25 local from Nottingham to Leicester which is seen leaving Ruddington on 2 March. No 44821 also worked a Leicester-Brighton excursion on 11 August 1958 the locomotive being used in both directions with Frank Stratford as fireman. *J. F. Henton*

Centre right:
The 17.20 Woodford 'ord' leaves Leicester Central with WR 'Hall' 4-6-0 No 6976 *Graythwaite Hall* heading back to its home depot at Banbury on 25 August 1960. The locomotive had worked down to Leicester with the Bournemouth-York service. *H. A. Gamble*

Bottom right:
'Black Five' No 44847 is turned on the Rossmore Road turntable at Marylebone. The latter still exists, but the huge goods warehouse behind the engine is sadly no longer with us. 2 April 1965.
P. H. Wells

Facing page, top:
Colwick's 'L1' 2-6-4T No 67745 is pictured at Rothley station with the 17.30 Nottingham Victoria-Rugby on 15 August 1962.
D. Holmes

Facing page, bottom:
The 17.15 Nottingham Victoria-Marylebone semi-fast passes the plasterboard works at Hotchley Hill near Rushcliffe Halt on 19 May 1964. 'Black Five' No 44846 has its cylinder cocks open and, by the look of the exhaust, is priming badly. *M. Mitchell*

Facing page, top:
Well turned out 'Director' 4-4-0 No 62666 *Zeebrugge* pulls away from Sheffield Victoria with a local train for Nottingham Victoria on 19 April 1957.
K. S. Hudson

Top left:
'Royal Scot' 4-6-0 No 46156 minus nameplates passes the disused Rushcliffe Halt just north of East Leake with the 03.40 ex-Marylebone on 9 May 1964. This train took 5hr 3min for the 126 miles run! *J. S. Hancock*

Centre left:
East Leake station recedes into the distance, as 'Jubilee' No 45557 *New Brunswick* enters the deep cutting with the 17.15 Nottingham Victoria-Marylebone in September 1963. *J. S. Hancock*

Facing page, bottom:
BR Standard '5' 4-6-0 No 73053, still equipped with a chime whistle (which these locomotives lost as they went through shops), is pictured on the turntable road at Leicester Central on 6 July 1964, prior to taking over the 'Fish'. *M. Mitchell*

Left:
Leicester boasted many cross-country services and summer excursions. 'B16' No 61420 leaves Leicester Central on an empty stock working to the carriage sidings after arriving from Scarborough on 6 August 1965. *J. F. Henton*

Left:
The 14.38 Marylebone-Nottingham semi-fast leaves Rugby on 24 April 1965 with 'Black Five' No 45215 in charge.
M. Mensing

Below left:
'Black Five' No 45292 ascends Shawell Bank between Rugby and Lutterworth with the 12.30(SO) Rugby-Nottingham Victoria local on 11 September 1965.
M. Mitchell

Bottom:
Charwelton's once-thriving iron ore traffic is still in evidence on 16 June 1962 as 'Britannia' No 70015 *Apollo* runs through with the 16.38 Marylebone-Nottingham, before the semi-fasts were reduced to four coaches.
Ian Allan Library

Top:
In its first coat of paint, brand new BR Standard '5' No 73157 rushes through Woodford with the down 'Master Cutler' on 27 May 1957. *M. Mitchell*

Right:
The 10.28 Marylebone-Woodford 'ord' nears Helmdon in the care of 'B1' 4-6-0 No 61186 on 11 June 1962. *M. Mitchell*

Right:
**'Britannia' Pacific
No 70033 *Charles Dickens*
arrives at Ashby Magna
with the 14.38 from
Marylebone on 6 August
1963.** *G. D. King*

Below right:
**'B1' 4-6-0 No 61051 storms
past Bagthorpe Junction
signalbox with a Swansea-
York express on 8 August
1959.** *J. F. Henton*

Bottom:
**Woodford 'B1' No 61078
returns to her home depot
from Marylebone with an
evening local in July
1958.** *G. C. Farnell*

Top:
Forerunner of the 'B1s' No 61000 _Springbok_ is seen at Marylebone in September 1961. As the locomotive bears no shed plate, this was probably after its transfer to Colwick shed where it resided until withdrawal in March 1962. The locomotive had worked a long distance 'ord' from Leicester. _G. C. Farnell_

Above right:
One of the five BR Standard '5' 4-6-0s that went brand new to Neasden when built. No 73159 is pictured in rather dirty condition at Aylesbury with the 08.15 Nottingham-Marylebone in September 1959. _G. C. Farnell_

Right:
The 08.15 semi-fast is seen again — this time in the charge of 'Black Five' No 45215 at Aylesbury in April 1961. _G. C. Farnell_

Left:
The 16.50 'South Yorkshireman' from Marylebone to Bradford gets away from Aylesbury behind 'A3' Pacific No 60102 *Sir Frederick Banbury* **in October 1958. Note the fine clear exhaust denoting a good fire.**
N. Stead

Below:
The 08.30 Manchester-Marylebone express tears towards the Chilterns and Wendover with 'B1' No 61380 in charge in July 1958. *G. C. Farnell*

3

Belgrave Road — a Leicester Outpost

The Great Northern line to Leicester Belgrave Road meandered from the East Midlands areas (from the Nottingham to Grantham line) and the East Coast Main Line at Peterborough, through sparsely populated countryside and, not surprisingly, attracted few passengers. By 1953 there were only three trains per day between Melton and Market Harborough. Belgrave Road once had services to many destinations — all were hopelessly uneconomic and by 1950 just two trains a day ran from Leicester to Grantham — the 10.30 'express' departure connecting with the down 'Flying Scotsman' at Grantham. September 1951 saw the demise of this, and only the 07.35 Melton to Leicester, with the 18.10 return, ran during the week with an extra Saturday service for shoppers.

February 1953 saw BR's announcement of the intention to end all services, not surprising as Tilton only averaged two passengers per day, and only 67 passengers regularly used the service. The annual loss was £29,000. However, a large and amazing local campaign, insistent that the local communities depended on the line, ensued to thwart closure. Despite the last train on 5 December 1953, two unadvertised services continued to run from Leicester to John O'Gaunt and from Market Harborough to East Norton. Belgrave Road's main traffic now consisted of weekend excursion trains. The power for these services was usually provided by GNR 0-6-0 locomotives and later the 'B1' 4-6-0s. The track was in a less than good condition and speeds were slow until the

Right:
Route map illustrating the position of Leicester Belgrave Road station relative to other lines.

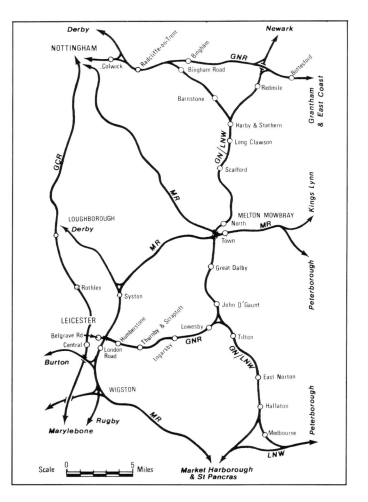

Above:
'B1' 4-6-0 No 61163 is pictured after arriving at Leicester Belgrave Road station with the 13.52 from Mablethorpe on Saturday 9 September 1961. *H. A. Gamble*

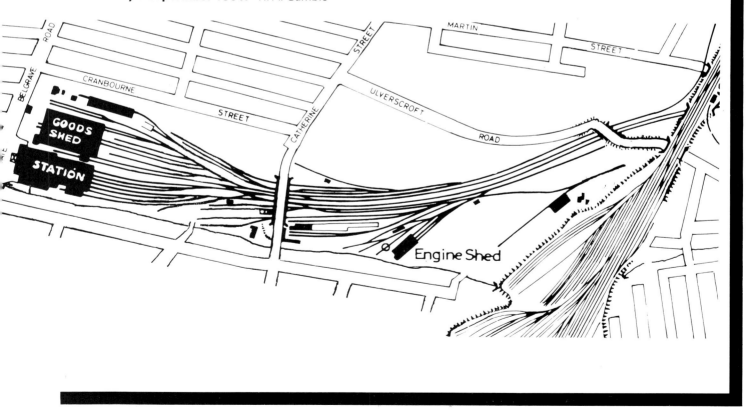

Grantham line was reached. The GNR 0-6-0s also handled freight trains — though very few — and were often in tremendous trouble over the steep grades of the line. It is amazing to think that in 1959 20,000 people travelled from Belgrave Road in 72 trains to Mablethorpe and Skegness in true holiday style. Out of town stops were made at Humberstone and Thurnby. Where do these people go now? The site of Belgrave Road station is now a roundabout on a new municipal motorway in Leicester. The end of summer 1962 was therefore not just the end of a line but the end of an era.

Frank Stratford
Working the line

Although not strictly of GC lineage, mention must now be made of Leicester Central's small outpost at Leicester Belgrave Road. This was the terminus of the one time GNR branch, and was worked by men in the No 3 link, the bottom main line link, so as a young passed cleaner one encountered the work there quite regularly. By this time the Saturdays-only train to Grantham had been discontinued. This left only the morning workman's train from Melton Mowbray to Leicester, and the corresponding evening return train. These were both all-station jobs, and the passengers from the remote stations such as Ingarsby and Lowesby were few and far between.

In the morning we used to go light engine to Melton Mowbray, pick up the two coaches and work to Leicester. We were then booked 'engine and brake van' to Stathern and Bottesford where we shunted the yards and worked back with timber, petrol and other goods for Leicester. After working the evening passenger train and depositing the stock in Melton yard, we returned light engine with our guard who, additionally, during the winter months had to stop and blow out all the oil lamps at every station.

Some funny things used to happen that would be unheard of on many lines. For instance, on one occasion, a certain Leicester crew derailed the coaches in Melton yard, so were stuck for a train to work the few regular clients to Leicester. Not wanting to let the passengers down, the guard discovered a goods brake van was handy so they actually worked the passengers to Leicester with that.

The freight jobs consisted of the Leicester goods yard shunt, the Bottesford pick-up and a night goods to Colwick, returning with the early morning freight to Leicester. This was a very heavily loaded train in both directions, and really taught you your trade as a fireman. The coal had to be broken up small and the engines fired six shovels at a time with a thin fire. The line out of Leicester climbs sharply and, if the engine started slipping, you could take about an hour to get up to Mirfield Junction, a distance of some 10 miles. There were even stories of men walking in front of the train to sand the rails! The staple power was the GNR 'J5s' and 'J6s' with sometimes a GC 'J11' or Gresley 'J39'.

On the freight trains, or when running 'engine and brake', it was not unusual to stop and pick mushrooms. At the small signalbox of Stathern Ironstone sidings, a certain signalman called Harold ran a thriving market garden business and the box was always full of fruit and vegetables of all description. He would take orders for any amount of fruit, and we often used to arrive back with the footplate loaded down with produce for the men at the depot.

One of the big problems with loose-coupled freight trains and small engines was the control of the train on steep down gradients. The early morning return from Colwick was nearly always loaded to the maximum and many a time I've come down the gradient on tenterhooks wondering if my mate would manage to stop in time. Just outside Belgrave Road was Forest Road level crossing and a certain signalman who rejoiced in the pseudonym of 'Double Blank' was often to be found asleep, and we would be hanging on the whistle, making a noise that would wake the dead as we neared the crossing gates. In fact, more than one driver was known to have lengthened the arrival road by hitting the stop blocks! During the summer months the passenger work was greatly augmented by the running of expresses to Skegness and Mablethorpe on Saturdays and Sundays. At one time these were all worked by Leicester men and, on good days, duplicates would also be run. If you were lucky you had a 'big' engine — ie, a 'K2' 2-6-0, but otherwise it was the usual 'J6' 0-6-0.

I was lucky enough to work one of the 'Evening Cruise' trains in September 1954 with Driver Sid Parker. Our engine was a newly out-shopped 'K2' No 61771 and we enjoyed a really good trip to 'Skeggy'. On this occasion a duplicate also followed us, with a 'J6' as power. Unfortunately, the duplicate ran before us on the return trip and they got into all sorts of trouble, stopping short of steam. We were standing behind them blowing off steam but unable to do anything but keep waiting for them to clear the section in front. We arrived at Belgrave Road about three hours late and the looks of the passengers who had missed connecting buses home had to be seen to be believed. Unfortunately, I went into the army in early 1955 and thereby missed a summer season on the east coast trains. When I returned in 1957, the jobs had been taken over by Colwick men with the resulting 30-mile tender first light engine running after each trip.

The depot at Belgrave Road was a small three-road affair which usually housed about four engines, but this total could sometimes almost double on summer weekends. There was a mechanical foreman, Fred Mould, in charge of the shed, with a steam raiser to attend to the engines on each of three shifts. This meant that from 10 o'clock at night until the first set of enginemen came on at 04.30, the steam raiser was on his own. This was one duty we would often be booked to work as 16-year-old passed cleaners, and what with the local householders sneaking over to top up their coal houses, it could be a harrowing experience.

As stated previously, the jobs were worked by Leicester Central's No 3 link. There were four different turns of duty. The first set of men came on at 04.30, prepared the engine for the Melton/Bottesford job and also prepared their own engine to work the goods yard shunt. The second set at 06.15 worked light engine up to Melton Mowbray, brought the workmen's train into Leicester, and then went 'engine and brake' to Bottesford to work the pick-up goods.

There was then an afternoon turn at 14.45 which disposed and turned the engine returning from Bottesford and worked the 18.10 to Melton, returning light engine. The last set of men came on at 20.35 and worked the goods to Colwick. This was always a very heavily loaded train and, as stated previously, some mighty struggles up the bank ensued. The

Left:
'B1' 4-6-0 No 61285 leaves
Belgrave Road in fine style
with a Skegness train on
6 August 1962. *G. D. King*

men on duty at 14.45 had to wait until the signalman at Belgrave Road rang to inform them that the goods was safely past the junction at Mirfield before they could sign off duty.

The motive power for the line was all supplied by Colwick shed and consisted mostly of 'J6' 0-6-0s, all of GN parentage, supplanted by GC 'J11s' and, if one was very lucky, a Gresley 'J39'. In the summer the big engines used to arrive — the 'K2' 2-6-0s for the East Coast trains. Ironically, when Colwick men took over the working of the trains, they had the luxury of 'B1' 4-6-0s — a pleasure never enjoyed by Leicester men. Minor repairs were carried out by Fred Mould, but everything else was performed by Colwick so the engines would be changed on a regular basis as they became due for boiler washing out.

The final job worked by Leicester men, after the shed closed, was to relieve the one remaining goods train in the morning from Colwick, shunt the yard and prepare the train for Colwick men who would travel out and work the train back to Colwick. (In fact, in July 1963 I was booked on this turn with 'B1' No 61264 — now the subject of a preservation project at Loughborough.) Even after the branch closed, Belgrave Road yard remained open for freight for a few more years being connected by a spur to the Midland main line at Humberstone. As late as 1966, I shunted there with an '08' diesel shunter.

One unusual happening took place at Belgrave Road shed on a nice summer's day in 1957. Driver Sid Parker and his mate were sitting out in the sun enjoying a cup of tea after disposing of the engine off the Bottesford train. Suddenly, there was an ominous rumbling sound and a huge cloud of dust shot up over the shed. On investigation, they discovered that the main part of the roof had collapsed and they had to remove a large quantity of beams and planks that had buried two 'J6s'! It was never repaired and Belgrave Road shed retained a 'sunshine roof' until its demise.

LEICESTER (BELGRAVE ROAD) TO MABLETHORPE AND SKEGNESS (15 JUNE to 13 SEPTEMBER 1959)

		Weekdays		Sundays
		(SO)	(SO)	
Leicester (Belgrave Road)	d	08.22	09.10	09.45
Humberstone	d	08.29	09.17	09.51
Thurnby & Scraptoft	d	08.35	09.23	09.57
Melton Mowbray North	a	09.04	09.52	10.24
	d	09.08	09.56	10.28
Bottesford	d		10.26	
Boston	d	10.42	11.30	
Skegness	a	11.25	12.34	12.27
Sutton-on-Sea	a	11.39	12.23	
Mablethorpe	a	11.47	12.31	

MABLETHORPE AND SKEGNESS TO LEICESTER (BELGRAVE ROAD) (15 JUNE to 13 SEPTEMBER 1959)

		Weekdays		Sundays
		(SO)	(SO)	
Mablethorpe	d		13.52	
Sutton-on-Sea	d		14.00	
Skegness	d	13.32		19.34
Boston	d	14.17	14.45	
Bottesford	d		15.48	
Melton Mowbray North	a	15.50	16.16	21.36
	d	15.54	16.20	21.41
Thurnby & Scraptoft	a	16.26	16.56	22.09
Humberstone	a	16.31	17.01	22.16
Leicester (Belgrave Road)	a	16.36	17.06	22.21

Right:
The 09.20 from Leicester Belgrave Road with 'B1' 4-6-0 No 61142 in charge, calls at Humberstone, to pick up passengers for 'Skeggy' on 7 August 1961. *H. A. Gamble*

Below right:
'B1' No 61232 storms away from Leicester over Forest Road crossing with the 10.10 Belgrave Road-Skegness on Sunday 29 July 1962. *P. H. Wells*

Bottom:
A Belgrave Road to Colwick freight is pictured under the glassless roof at Melton Mowbray North, with power provided by one of the staple movers on the branch — 'J6' 0-6-0 No 64269 on 4 July 1959. *B. O. Hilton*

Left:
'B1' 4-6-0 No 61177 simmers at Leicester Belgrave Road after bringing in the 13.32 from Skegness on 29 August 1959. The site of Belgrave Road station is now a roundabout.
P. J. Shoesmith

Below left:
'B1' No 61177 is seen passing Melton Mowbray North on its journey to Leicester Belgrave Road from Skegness on 29 August 1959.
P. J. Shoesmith

Bottom:
A Mablethorpe-Leicester service with 'B1' No 61390 at its head runs through derelict Lowesby station on the 27 August 1960. The state of the track should be noted. It is amazing to think that services were still allowed over such a decrepit route. *J. S. Spencer*

4

Express Passenger Workings

Robert Robotham

Manchester to Marylebone — the main line

Leicester Central was very much the centre of the Great Central main line passenger service. The normal weekday service saw, in the down direction, the 01.45 'Newspaper', the 10.00, 12.15 and 15.20 to Manchester London Road — the 12.15 was routed via the GW/GC joint line through Princes Risborough — while the 'South Yorkshireman' for Bradford left London at 16.50 and the 'Master Cutler' followed it at 18.18. The last express was the 22.00 Marylebone to Manchester and Liverpool mail. To London ran the 'Master Cutler' (07.40 Sheffield-Marylebone), the 08.30 Manchester-Marylebone, the 'South Yorkshireman', (10.00 Bradford-Marylebone), followed by the 14.10 and 16.05 workings from Manchester to Marylebone. The Liverpool and Manchester up mail went at 21.30. These expresses stopped at Leicester to change engines and crews and, until 1954, the crews ran northwards as far as Manchester. After the electrification of the Manchester-Sheffield route, Sheffield became the limit of steam working. Some services had many stops en route which involved fast rousing starts and screeching stops. This technique was perfected by the GC locomen and was unequalled anywhere on British Railways.

Right:
BR Standard '5' 4-6-0 No 73000 was a regular GC locomotive and is seen at Neasden shed when brand new. As the date is 25 April 1951, one would assume it had been on exhibition at Marylebone. In its later years No 73000 was shedded at Woodford. *C. C. B. Herbert*

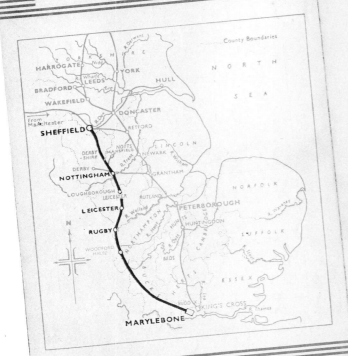

THE
MASTER
CUTLER

LONDON (MARYLEBONE)
RUGBY
LEICESTER NOTTINGHAM
SHEFFIELD (VICTORIA)

SEPTEMBER 26th, 1949
until further notice

RESTAURANT CAR TRAIN

The cover (above) and inside (below) of the handbill produced in 1949 to advertise the 'Master Cutler' service.

· THE MASTER CUTLER ·

THE name of Sheffield is synonymous with cutlery, and the history of its ancient Cutlers Company, or to use its correct designation, the Master, Wardens, Searchers, Assistants and Commonalty of the Company of Cutlers in Hallamshire in the County of York, is full of interest

The first Parliamentary Act incorporating the Company was passed in 1624. By long-established custom, the installation of the Master Cutler is a ceremonial occasion of great dignity. The new Master takes an oath of loyalty to the Throne and of obligation to his duties, and is then inducted by his predecessor. The Wardens, Searchers and Assistants are duly sworn in, and the assembly proceeds to the Cathedral Church

The continued excellence of Sheffield products is largely due to the long tradition of skilled workmanship so zealously guarded by the Cutlers Company. The Company has always stood for the protection and development of all that is best in the highly specialised cutlery, steel and edged tool industries. In the past it has regulated conditions of apprenticeship and employment, as well as preserving quality standards, and controlling widely different questions of trade custom. It still maintains its authority in the use and registration of Trade Marks, and the safeguarding of the name of Sheffield

The Master Cutler train gives expression to the close link between British Railways and the city of Sheffield, and symbolises the tradition of strength and excellence upheld by the Cutlers Company

WEEKDAYS

Sheffield (Victoria)	...	dep.	a.m. 7 40
Nottingham (Victoria)	...	{ arr. dep.	8 35 8 38
Leicester (Central)	...	{ arr. dep.	9 6 9 10
Rugby (Central)	...	{ arr. dep.	9 36 9 38
LONDON (Marylebone)	...	arr.	11 15

LONDON (Marylebone)	...	dep.	p.m. 6 15
Rugby (Central)	...	{ arr. dep.	8 4 8 6
Leicester (Central)	...	{ arr. dep.	8 29 8 34
Nottingham (Victoria)	...	{ arr. dep.	9 0 9 4
Sheffield (Victoria)	...	arr.	9 58

RESERVATION OF SEATS
Seats can be reserved in advance at Sheffield (Victoria) and Marylebone on payment of a fee of 1/- per seat

Frank Stratford

Working the trains

The working of express passenger turns with steam engines required a certain technique and Leicester men were justly proud of their time keeping record. The depot's work consisted mostly of passenger turns, so firemen were brought up from an early age to know what was expected of them. It was imperative to keep the steam pressure near to the 'red mark', to enable the driver to notch up the cut-off, thereby working the engine as economically as possible. If the steam pressure was allowed to drop, the engine would get progressively weaker and the driver would have to work it harder to keep time, so a good team effort was required. Working expresses continuously was skilled and very hard work. This was brought home to Annesley men when, after a lifetime working freight trains, they were suddenly presented with the diverted Manchester-London sleeper which was routed over the GC section during electrification of the LNWR main line. Marylebone men who used to relieve them on the up train at Leicester would regularly have a 10min 'blow-up' to get the steam pressure round and boiler full before departing for London.

On Mondays only, it was Leicester men who relieved the up train, and I well remember one morning waiting to relieve the train. My mate asked the signalman where the train had got to and, after being told that it had passed Loughborough, we waited another 45min for the train to cover the 10 miles! It finally limped into Leicester in a terrible state with 120lb of steam pressure and the water level barely visible in the gauge glass. I looked into the firebox to check that the lead plugs were not blowing and was staggered at the sight. The air scoop had been taken out of the firehole and there was even coal on top of the brick arch. After a bit of work with the fire irons, the replacement of the air scoop and about 10min preparation we had a full boiler and full head of steam and set off for Marylebone with BR Standard '5' No 73045 — never experiencing one moment of trouble all the way.

Leicester men could not understand such goings on as just mentioned, as they were used to dashing from Loughborough in slightly less than 45min. On a 'run through', the pass-to-stop time from Loughborough to Leicester was about 8½min. The really hard timing was on the up expresses that called at Loughborough. The 10 miles to Leicester had to be run from a standing start on the foot of the bank in just 11min! While there were a few old drivers who would not even try to do it, saying it was crazy, most of the men at Leicester, especially the younger element among the drivers, used to revel in it, vying with each other to try and get within the magic 'even time' of 10min.

With 'Radar' Ron Smith, we used to do the time regularly, although some of the 'elite' enginemen would have winced at our methods. I used to continue firing the engine all the way down the bank from Barnstone tunnel so that, on arrival at Loughborough, we would have a box full of fire that Ron could 'remove' up the chimney to Leicester. Ron used to wait with his hand on the regulator for my shout of 'Right away' as I relayed the guard's signal to him. The regulator would be yanked right across and with the steam sanders on we would blast our way under the overbridges in a cacophony of sound and cinders as we made for Quorn & Woodhouse which you

had to pass in roughly 3min or you had not got much chance. Ron used to wind the cut-off up only one nick at a time as we hammered up the bank and we would probably never be any higher than 45% cut-off for the whole journey! We would keep steam on until somewhere in the region of Abbey Lane box, a staggering thought really to think that we would be still doing somewhat more than 80mph with the station only a mile away. Ron would then do a 'GC stop' — ie, a full brake application — and, with the brakes squealing, we would shoot around the curves into the platform at rather more than the regulation 25mph! After grinding to a halt, the engine would immediately be wound into backgear and 'eased up' for the shunter to uncouple and, after placing a head lamp on to the tender lamp iron, we would rush off to the shed. There was no hanging about, as from arrival to departure, including the engine change, expresses were only allowed 4min at Leicester. The 'B1s' seemed to be the best on the 'mad 10min', but Ron and I achieved the time with numerous different engines including 'Black Five' No 44932 (now preserved at Steamtown), Standard '5s', '9Fs' and one glorious trip when we flailed a 'K3' home in 10min.

I can understand in a way the men who would not try the timing, as they pointed out, odd minutes could have been taken off between Sheffield and Nottingham and minutes added to the Loughborough-Leicester schedule. Men like Ron Smith though always worked to the practice of 'A timetable's a timetable', and would do their utmost to run to time. I must admit that I hated to run late and never enjoyed being with a driver who did not care about his time keeping.

Luckily, most of my time on passenger work was spent with Ron Smith and we would regularly try everything possible to get the trains there to time. For example, one night on 2 April 1960, we were working back from Sheffield with the Swindon Mail and, due to engineering works on the main line, we were to be diverted via the LDEC route from Killamarsh to Kirkby South Junction. As Leicester men had not at this time learned the road over this route, we were blessed with a Darnall Pilot Driver. As he boarded our steed (Standard '5' No 73066), he remarked that such an engine would never run this heavy train to time. He set off in true 'grinder' fashion, thrashing the engine along, as he was worried about dropping time. Imagine his surprise to find he was 10min early at Kirkby South Junction! Alas, his thrashing had been all to no avail for, as we free-wheeled down to Annesley South, we were met by adverse signals due to a points failure. We eventually left there 5min late and, owing to very heavy mail traffic at Nottingham Victoria, left there 10min late. Nevertheless, with a bit of shrewd management, we still effected a 'right time' arrival in Leicester. On another occasion, Sunday 19 June 1960, whilst working an afternoon express to London with 'B1' No 61090, we arrived at Aylesbury to find a minor calamity. The fireman had failed to arrive for the 'all stations' which followed 10min behind us from Aylesbury. The plan now was that we would wait for 10min, run as the local as far as Rickmansworth, and then take up our own working from there. A passenger came up in an agitated state as he had a plane to catch from Heathrow. Ron said he would do his best and we blasted out of Aylesbury hell-bent on running to time. I was kept busy on the shovel and, with smart work by our guard at the stops, we managed to run our nine coaches along in fine style. The end product of our hard work was a

2min late arrival in Marylebone. The aforesaid passenger actually thanked Ron for his work but unfortunately heard me say under my breath 'We can't buy ale on thanks'. As he departed, he gave us a withering look but no tip!

Another top link driver who usually arrived on time was Leicester's Len Woodhead. In fact in October 1963 a week with Len on the 00.30 sleeper from Marylebone produced the following at Leicester:

Weekday	Locomotive No	Arrival
Monday	46125	Right time
Tuesday	46122	8½min early
Wednesday	46156	7min early
Thursday	46156	7min early
Friday	46156	Right time

Unfortunately, Driver Alf Scott and I really blotted our copybook on the Saturday by running 20min late with run-down Annesley 'Black Five' No 45285!

Another hard stretch to work over was the Chesterfield branch in the up direction. From a start at Chesterfield it was all 'against the collar' until after rejoining the main line at Heath Junction. To compound matters, the route consisted almost entirely of twists and turns with hardly a straight length of rail on the branch. This was another stretch of line where the 'bark' of an engine was heard to good effect.

The two named trains on the GC the 'Master Cutler' and the 'South Yorkshireman', were worked for most of their length by Leicester men. The 'Cutler' was worked throughout on the up journey from Sheffield to Marylebone by a Leicester engine and crew. The down train was worked from Marylebone to Leicester by Neasden men who uncoupled and returned light engine to London. A Leicester engine and crew worked forward to Sheffield. The 'South Yorkshireman' was also worked from Sheffield to Marylebone by Leicester engines and crews with the men who worked from Leicester to Marylebone returning with the corresponding down train. This then went forward from Leicester with a set of Darnall men and a Bradford Low Moor 'Black Five'. The men were very proud of these trains and always tried to run them to time or regain any time not lost through their own fault. The normal power was an 'A3' Pacific, or later a 'V2' 2-6-2 but the men would cheerfully take a 'B1' without complaining, as most of the ones at Leicester were well maintained for the job. Assisting engines were virtually unheard of on the GC section, but it was very rare to hear of much time being lost that the guard could legitimately book as 'Loco'.

I remember Ken Davis, one of the renowned Leicester 'Fliers', once telling me about a trip on the up 'Cutler' when, after leaving Leicester 14min late with 'V2' No 60879 (in my humble opinion possibly the best 'V2' Leicester had), they actually recovered it all and arrived in Marylebone on time. Unbeknown to Ken, riding in the train was one of his fellow drivers, Len Woodhead. Both agreed that the pass-to-pass time from Culworth Junction to Grendon Junction, a distance of 20 miles, was a little over 16min! Ken admitted to me that the lurching and rolling of the engine as they 'dive bombed' down through Brackley and round the curves over the viaduct, was a little bit unnerving! This typifies the sort of men on the GC. My father, who operated a water mill on the River Soar, never owned a watch, but timed himself for

dinner breaks by the trains that passed on the GC and would rarely be late home for a meal.

The motive power on the GC section which, when I began my career, consisted mostly of Eastern Region locomotives, changed considerably over the years. The well loved 'A3' Pacifics dominated the express services but were later replaced by 'V2' 2-6-2s also well liked by GC men for their good steaming and hill-climbing capabilities. The ubiquitous 'B1' 4-6-0s were to be found on everything from pick-ups to expresses but were themselves gradually replaced by 'Black Fives' and BR Standard types as the line succumbed to London Midland Region influence. As a fireman I worked on all these types as well as 'K3s', 'B16s', 'L1' tanks and Midland 'Jubilees'. I have read and heard over the years many arguments relating to 'B1' versus 'Black Five' and, from a purely operating point of view, I would like to throw in my 'two penn'orth'.

Both engines had their good and bad points but for steaming, fast running and good injectors, the 'B1' would come out on top. The 'B1' failed though when due for overhaul, as their riding qualities were appalling. They used to rattle and bang and knock terribly in the axleboxes and to experience No 61028 *Umseke* or No 61008 *Kudu* when really run down, made one wonder how they did not simply fall to pieces. GC men would put up with this to an extent though, as they steamed well, and even on a poor-steaming example, one could let the boiler level drop knowing that when the driver shut off you could slam on the live steam injector and soon fill the boiler up.

However, this was not the case with the 'Black Five'. Why is it that Stanier built a good sturdy workmanlike engine and then saddled it with an abberation of an injector? The normal function of an injector is to deliver water from the tank to the boiler. On most 'Black Fives' the exhaust steam injectors delivered 50% of the water on to the sleeper ends. Also the change-over valves used to stick so that when the driver shut off steam or opened the regulator, they would blow off. Thus the fireman had to shut the injector off and start again slowly. Resorting to the live steam injector on the driver's side did not really improve matters, as the minute the driver applied the brake and the water surged in the tank, off would blow this injector also. The problems were compounded if the injector clack valve stuck up. In the rare event of a clack sticking on an Eastern Region engine, one just picked up a spanner and screwed in the clack on the face plate. On the 'Black Five' the top feed was set on the top of the boiler, and with Mr Stanier having built his engines with no running plate round the cabside, one could not get out on to the top framing to screw the clack down until the engine was stationary!

Stanier's Class 4 2-6-4Ts were also very prone to injectors blowing off when braking for station stops, and more than once No 42437 had to have the fire thrown out en route due to injector clacks sticking and the water level dropping too low in the boiler. The method we devised to get around this was to wait until the train stopped in the station before using the injector. The tender water feeds on Stanier tenders were also prone to drop open, thereby wasting water, and one soon learned to wedge a lump of coal behind them to keep them closed. No wonder there were water troughs 'every two bogie lengths' on the LNWR main line!

Returning to the riding qualities of the engines, I well remember a trip from Sheffield with 'B1' No 61085 with Inspector Percy Banyard on the footplate. The engine was overdue for shopping and in a terrible condition. Percy reported the vibration as being so bad as to be giving the crew a distorted view of signals through the cab lookouts. The engine went to Doncaster works and, apart from No 61057 which was condemned in 1950 after collision damage, became the first 'B1' to be scrapped in normal service, as early as November 1961.

The third engines in the Class 5 category to arrive at Leicester were the BR Standards in the 73000 series. Apart from a few of the old hand drivers who could not see any good in anything else but a GC engine, the Standard '5s' were well-liked by all the men who worked them. Personally, I preferred them to any other 4-6-0s I had worked on. They were good steamers, good pullers, the injectors were superb and they rode 'like a coach' in railwaymen's parlance. In his otherwise excellent book on the Stanier 4-6-0s, J. W. P. Rowledge lists the Standard '5s' along with the 842 'Black Fives' built. This does not hold water with me, as I had 422 trips on 70 different 'Black Fives' as a fireman, and not one of these could compare with a Standard. Paper talk means nothing to a man who has to run the trains to time — the performance of his engine is what counts. To me, the Standards were nothing remotely like a 'Black Five' but much more like an Eastern Region engine, with their motion, riding and good injectors. It was easily possible to get through from Leicester to London on a tank of water without taking a 'dip' on Charwelton troughs with a Standard, but you would be hard pushed to try it with a 'Black 'un'. To finalise it, if there were two engines to work a job, a 'B1' and a 'Black Five', both of equal riding and steaming ability, and the shed foreman gave me a choice, I would opt for the 'B1' simply because of the reliability of the injectors. If a third engine was added to the choice, being a Standard, then I would unhesitatingly opt for the latter every time.

Not much in the way of unusual motive power was found on the GC line expresses when the line was under the Eastern Region control. In the 1940s as a train spotter at Whetstone, I remember well the 'Footballer' ('B17') 4-6-0s that flew by.

These were then all transferred to the Great Eastern section, to be replaced by 'A3s', 'V2s' and 'B1s'. It was not unusual also, especially in the summertime with the extra holiday trains, to see the Gresley 'K3s' utilised on passenger work. Although only a small-wheeled engine compared to a 'B1', the 'jazzers' as the 'K3s' were known, were not bad engines and would run in the 70mph bracket. They suffered a bit in the riding department but, with their huge boilers, were very economical to run.

Things altered when the Midland Region were in charge of the motive power. Leicester Central was loaned a Caprotti Standard, No 73138. I thought it was a great engine, but after a certain crew had lost time on the 'South Yorkshireman' due to lack of steam it went to Derby for a boiler examination and never came back. We also received BR Standard '4' 4-6-0s of the 75000 series and the well-liked '9F' 2-10-0s. What a revelation the latter were on the GC expresses. They could not be used in the winter due to their lack of steam heating apparatus, but were seen on all the expresses in the summer season.

One of Leicester's 'fliers', Ken Davis was well known for his dash to Nottingham Victoria on the 'Cutler' with '9F' No 92164, but, well before this, on Whit Monday, 11 June 1962 Driver Ron Smith and myself whirled a Skegness special from Leicester to Nottingham in 23min! I do not know what speed we actually reached, but I remember looking out of the cab going down the bank through Rushcliffe Halt and the wheels and motion were just a blur! To do this stretch from start to stop in even time we certainly were not hanging about. I also experienced the '9Fs' on jobs such as the Mail from Sheffield Vic to Leicester and, even with 500 tons behind the drawbar, they would waltz up the bank from Staveley to Heath Junction 'as though you were running light engine', as one driver put it. The amusing finale to all this came when, after a full summer of dashing about with the '9Fs', a printed circular from head office was posted in the depot informing one and all that this class of engine was limited to 50mph and was only to be used on express work in an emergency! Still, it was great fun while it lasted and what a pity these marvellous machines never saw even half the life span one would have expected from a steam engine.

Left:
Long standing Leicester 'A3' No 60102 *Sir Frederick Banbury* **makes a fine sight as she runs through Aylesbury with the 07.40 Sheffield-Marylebone 'Master Cutler' in August 1951. The train was retimed to a 07.50 departure by June 1959, and the name transferred some months earlier to a new Pullman service that ran via Retford to King's Cross.**
G. C. Farnell

LEICESTER CENTRAL TO AYLESBURY

Service: 'South Yorkshireman'
Locomotives: [1] 'B1' No 61092 [2] 'B1' No 61298
Load Tons (Tare): [1] 254 [2] 318
Load Tons (Gross): [1] 270 [2] 340

			[1]		[2]	
Distance (miles)		*Schedule (minutes)*	*Actual (minutes/seconds)*	*Speeds (mph)*	*Actual (minutes/seconds)*	*Speeds (mph)*
0.0	Leicester		00.00	–	00.00	–
4.7	Whetstone		06.47	59	07.24	55
9.2	Ashby		11.51	51	13.17	44
13.1	Lutterworth		16.03	64	18.08	–
16.3	Shawell Signalbox		19.01	71	21.22	71
19.9	Rugby	24	22.46	–	25.01	–
4.7	Braunston		06.24	64	06.41	60
11.7	Charwelton		14.47	44	14.55	45
14.1	Woodford		17.44	50	17.42	60
15.8	Culworth Junction		20.00	44	19.15	69
20.7	Helmdon		25.09	–	23.05	59
23.9	Brackley		28.15	59	26.36	74
28.7	Finmere		32.32	72	30.37	82
34.4	Calvert		36.49	92	35.12	81
36.4	Grendon Junction		38.26	60*	36.55	60*
39.1	Quainton Road		41.16	–	39.43	–
45.2	Aylesbury	51	48.21	–	46.29	–

* Service slack   Source: O. S. Nock *Railway Magazine*

LONDON (MARYLEBONE) TO LEICESTER CENTRAL

Service: 'Master Cutler'
Locomotives: [1] BR Standard '5' No 73157 [2] 'B1' No 61083
Load Tons (Tare): [1] 316 [2] 376
Load Tons (Gross): [1] 330 [2] 395

		[1]		[2]		
Distance (miles)		*Minutes/ seconds*	*Speeds (mph)*	*Minutes/ seconds*	*Speeds (mph)*	*Schedule*
0.0	Marylebone	00.00	–	00.00	–	
3.0	Kilburn	07.34	29/57	07.46	27/53	
5.1	Neasden South Junction	10.17	38*	10.37	39*	
8.8	Sudbury Hill	15.05	48/60	15.30	45/57	
11.6	South Ruislip	18.37	38*	19.32	24*	
16.1	Denham	24.18	58	–	–	
18.7	Gerrards Cross	27.17	50	sigs	–	
23.0	Beaconsfield	31.26	52	stop and	–	
27.9	High Wycombe	37.40	37*	checks	–	
32.8	Saunderton	44.58	42	sigs	30	
		sigs	40*			
36.0	Princes Risborough	49.19	–	57.46	–	
41.4	Haddenham	54.27	72	63.14	70/68	
43.4	Ashendon Junction	57.54	–	66.39	72	
		–	–	pws	35*	
51.3	Grendon Junction	63.23	61	72.18	–	
53.3	Calvert	65.19	–	75.31	62	
59.0	Finmere	70.58	52	81.29	57	
63.8	Brackley	75.54	65	86.03	70	
67.0	Helmdon	79.24	54	89.13	59	
70.6	Culworth	82.49	73	92.31	72	
73.6	Woodford	85.22	–	95.06	–	

Distance (miles)		Minutes/seconds [1]	Speeds (mph) [1]	Minutes/seconds [2]	Speeds (mph) [2]	Schedule
76.0	Charwelton	87.36	62	97.33	60	
79.6	Staverton Road	pws	51*	pws	20*	
83.0	Braunston	95.29	–	106.56	55	
87.7	Rugby	101.03	–	112.37	–	110min
3.6	Shawell Signalbox	04.31	48	05.30	51	
6.8	Lutterworth	08.20	60/55	09.04	63/58	
10.7	Ashby Magna	12.17	–	12.41	75	
15.2	Whetstone	18.10	73	16.26	70	
18.9	Leicester South Goods	21.23	–	19.54	66	
19.9	Leicester Central	23.06	–	21.30	–	23min

* Speed restriction

LEICESTER CENTRAL TO NOTTINGHAM VICTORIA

	Service:	'Master Cutler'		'Master Cutler'		'Master Cutler'		'South Yorkshireman'		'South Yorkshireman'	
	Locomotive:	'A3' No 60059		'A3' No 60107		'V2' No 60863		'B1' No 61029		Stanier '5' No 45027	
	Load Tons (Tare):	312		314		314		372		372	
	Load Tons (Gross):	325		330		330		390		390	
Distance (miles)		Minutes/seconds	Speed (mph)	Minutes/seconds	Speed (mph)	Minutes/seconds	Speed (mph)	Minutes/seconds	Speed (mph)	Minutes/seconds	Speed (mph)
0.0	Leicester	0.00	–	0.00	–	0.00	–	0.00	–	0.00	–
2.2	Belgrave	4.07	50	4.46	42	4.27	46	4.43	42	5.03	38
5.0	Rothley	6.52	68	7.54	64	7.26	66	7.54	63	8.28	60
7.8	Quorn	9.10	79	10.20	75	9.52	74	10.27	69	11.05	70
9.9	Loughborough	10.40	81	11.55	80	11.28	79	12.14	74	12.52	67
12.9	MP 90	13.03	71	14.20	69	13.58	66	14.52	60	15.36	60
14.4	East Leake	14.21	75	15.39	72	15.20	71	16.23	64	17.04	67
16.8	Gotham Junction	16.12 pws	83 15*	17.30	85	17.16	80	18.26	77	19.00	81
19.0	Ruddington	18.30	–	19.00	85	18.57	78	20.14	69	20.38	81
21.9	MP 81	–	60	–	75	–	70	sigs	*	–	68
22.5	Arkwright Street	23.13	*	21.40	*	21.51	*	23.53	*	23.38	*
23.4	Nottingham Victoria	25.40	–	23.41	–	24.13	–	27.34	–	26.03	–
	Net time (min)	23	–	23	–	24	–	25	–	24	–

Source: C. J. Allen *Trains Illustrated*

Left:
'V2' 2-6-2 No 60879 approaches Aylesbury with an up express, the 07.40 Sheffield-Marylebone, on 24 January 1959. Aylesbury North's up distant signal can be seen at the rear of the train, as can the rail connection to the factory on the right of the engine.
M. Mitchell

LONDON MARYLEBONE TO SHEFFIELD, WEEKDAYS
(15 JUNE to 13 SEPTEMBER 1959)

		MX A		B	C	D	E	F	G	H	J	K
Marylebone	d		01.45		10.00	12.15		15.20	16.50	18.18		22.00
Aylesbury	d				11.01			16.22	17.49			23.09
Brackley	d					13.36		16.46				23.35
Woodford	a				11.33	13.49		16.58			21.38	23.48
	d	00.15			11.35	13.51		17.00			21.43	23.50
Rugby	a	00.36		03.38	11.54	14.10	15.47	17.19	18.41	20.06	22.04	00.11
	d	00.40		03.49	11.56	14.12	15.49	17.21	18.42	20.08	22.09	00.16
Leicester	a	01.02		04.12	12.16	14.34	16.11	17.41	19.03	20.28	22.31	00.38
	d	01.12		07.30	12.21	14.39	16.20	17.46	19.08	20.33	22.44	00.48
Loughborough	d	01.28		07.49	12.35	14.52	16.35	18.00			23.00	01.05
Nottingham	a	01.46		08.16	12.51	15.08	16.52	18.15	19.34	20.58	23.18	01.23
	d	02.01		08.20	12.54	15.12	16.56	18.18	19.38	21.00	23.33	01.36
Chesterfield	a			09.13	13.41	15.49						
	d			09.14	13.42	16.01						
Sheffield	a	03.08		09.48	14.20	16.27	18.00	19.20	20.42	22.01	00.38	02.43

A: From Swindon dep 21.40 to York arr 04.59
B: To Manchester London Road 10.50
C: To Manchester London Road 15.19
D: To Manchester London Road 17.40
E: From Bournemouth West dep 11.16 to Newcastle arr 21.23
F: To Manchester London Road arr 20.26
G: 'South Yorkshireman' to Bradford Exchange 22.25
H: To Manchester London Road arr 23.24
J: From Swindon dep 19.30
K: To Manchester London Road arr 03.56 and Liverpool Central arr 05.40

Left:
The 12.15 Marylebone-Manchester express is seen with 'A3' Pacific No 60102 *Sir Frederick Banbury* rounding Ashendon Junction on 27 August 1955. The up WR line from Banbury crossed over the GC tracks here. The 12.15 from Marylebone was the return working for Leicester men after working the up 'Master Cutler' to London. The down 'Cutler' also took this route and the train often got stuck behind a tardy 'King' or 'Castle' on the 18.10 Paddington-Birmingham Snow Hill express.
S. Creer

Left:
Sheffield Victoria station on 18 April 1956. The up 'South Yorkshireman' is about to be relinquished by 'Black Five' No 45101 and taken over by Leicester 'A3' No 60102 *Sir Frederick Banbury* for the run south. The 'A3' also has coaches that make up the residual portion of the train.
R. Hewitt

SHEFFIELD TO LONDON MARYLEBONE, WEEKDAYS
(15 JUNE to 13 SEPTEMBER 1959)

		A	B		C	D	E	F	G	H
Sheffield	d	00.09	00.23	07.50	09.31	11.36	12.01	15.11	17.03	20.39
Chesterfield	a								17.32	
Nottingham	a	01.07	01.25	08.47	10.33	12.36	13.04	16.10	18.15	21.36
	d	01.20	01.45	08.50	10.39	12.39	13.06	16.15	18.20	21.50
Loughborough	d	01.40			10.57	12.59			18.39	22.10
Leicester	a	01.54	02.17	09.15	11.09	13.12	13.35	16.41	18.50	22.23
	d	02.12	02.33	09.20	11.13	13.17	13.40	16.46	18.55	22.38
Rugby	a	02.37		09.42	11.39	13.41	14.05	17.09	19.18	23.05
	d	02.43		09.44	11.40	13.43	14.07	17.11	19.20	23.14
Woodford	a	03.06	03.19		12.01			17.31	19.40	23.37
	d	03.09	03.21		12.03		14.45	17.33	19.42	23.43
Brackley	d				12.18				19.54	
Aylesbury	d		04.00		12.42	14.34		18.06	20.17	
Marylebone	a		05.05	11.27	13.40	15.36		19.10	21.19	

A: From York dep 22.22 to Swindon arr 05.45
B: From Liverpool Central dep 21.30
C: From Manchester London Road dep 08.30
D: 'South Yorkshireman' from Bradford Exchange dep 10.00
E: From Newcastle dep 08.35 to Bournemouth West arr 18.50
F: From Manchester London Road dep 14.10
G: From Manchester London Road dep 16.05
H: From York dep 18.40 to Swindon arr 02.00

Above:
Chesterfield Central is visited by Darnall 'B1' 4-6-0 No 61312 with the 16.05 Manchester-Marylebone in May 1958.
N. Stead

Left:
'B1' No 61271 climbs the bank from Whetstone to Ashby Magna with the Sundays 10.10 Nottingham Victoria-Marylebone on 8 April 1962. *M. Mitchell*

Above:

BR '9F' 2-10-0 No 92069 from Annesley is providing power for the up 'South Yorkshireman' and threads the cutting between Kirkby South Junction and Annesley tunnel. '9Fs' were pioneered on expresses by the GC sheds and 80-90 mph speeds were common. *J. Cupit*

Left:

'Black Five' 4-6-0 No 45208 clatters over Weekday Cross Junction on its way out of Nottingham Victoria with a York-Bournemouth working. The reversed headboard on the engine is for the 'South Yorkshireman' which the engine will work back from Leicester to Bradford. The tender is lettered in the early BR style and the date is August 1953. *J. P. Wilson*

Top:
'A3' Pacific No 60059
***Tracery* is pictured with**
the 08.30 Manchester-
Marylebone express
between Chalfont and
Chorleywood. No 60059
was the first 'A3' to return
to Leicester, painted in BR
green and converted to left
hand drive, in the summer
of 1952.   *G. C. Farnell*

Above:
'B1' 4-6-0 No 61271 heads
north from Princes
Risborough towards
Ashendon Junction with
an excursion from
Wembley to Sheffield via
Leicester in April 1960.
Note that the train is now
formed of London Midland
Region stock.   *G. C. Farnell*

Left:
'B1' 4-6-0 No 61008 *Kudu*
is going well with the up
'South Yorkshireman' near
Wendover in January
1959.   *G. C. Farnell*

49

5

The 3.20 Down

Frank Stratford

It is a nice autumn day in early October 1957. On the turntable road at Marylebone, under the Rossmore Road Bridge, 'B1' 4-6-0 No 61008 *Kudu* is standing quietly after being turned and watered, having arrived in London with the 8.30am train from Manchester. To the uninitiated the Kudu is a fleet-footed member of the South African fauna. The Leicester crew are relaxing after eating their 'snap', enjoying a few quiet moments before their dash back northwards with the 3.20 down. The driver is reading a paper and the fireman now leaves the footplate to carry out a most important function — making a fresh can of tea for consumption on the return trip. After his return to the cab with the 'brew', it is approaching 2.30, so the fireman now leaves the cab again to 'ring-off'. '3.20 engine bobby' is his short comment, which the signalman answers with an equally short 'OK Leicester'.

There is the squeal of a signal wire and the 'dolly' on the ground revolves to the 'off' position. The fireman climbs back aboard, and the driver moves his engine out on to the slow road and over the points, where another ground disc signal eventually calls us back into the platform. We are coupling up to our train in good time, as the steam heating is now in operation, and our 10 bogies will be well warmed up before our departure time. After placing the headlamps for express train code, the fireman begins a gradual build up of his fire, as 'Charley' Drake (the smoke inspector) will soon be reporting the crew if too much smoke appears over Marylebone. The fireman has allowed the water level in the boiler to drop to half a glass, so that as the steam pressure builds up, he can now use the live steam injector to control the pressure when it nears the blow-off point, as blowing off in termini is as bad

a fault as producing black smoke. Whilst the injector is on, the fireman has washed down the coal on the tender with the hose to try and control the dust, which is quite a problem at times on the B1s.

The guard arrives to inform the driver that his load is '10 for three three eight' (10 coaches making a total 338 tons), and the driver now tries his vacuum brake to ensure that after application, it will recreate and hold 21in of mercury on the gauge. All is now ready for departure with everything to the crew's satisfaction. The time is approaching 3.20pm. The platform starter signal is already raised in readiness for the departure of the train to Manchester. A shrill whistle sounds on the platform. 'Right away mate' says the fireman. The driver eases open the regulator. There is a metallic 'clunk' as the snifting valve behind the chimney closes and the train inches forward out of the platform. There are no engines to bank us out as happens at some termini, so the regulator is wide open as soon as the engine has settled without slipping.

The staccato bark from No 61008's chimney is now heard to good effect as we cross over the canal bridge and forge past Marylebone Goods signalbox and head our 10 coaches into the Lords tunnels. The fireman is now busy 'giving her a round' as we have a fair bit of climbing in front of us. There is a short length of daylight between the tunnels as we look down on the LNWR main lines, with South Hampstead station directly below our tracks. We burst into the sunlight past the small signal cabin at Canfield Place and on our right we are now joined by the Metropolitan electric tracks. The speed now builds up as we breast the summit and the driver has notched up the cut-off, but the regulator has not been eased as we clatter over Neasden South Junction, as there is still a fair climb to Harrow-on-the-Hill.

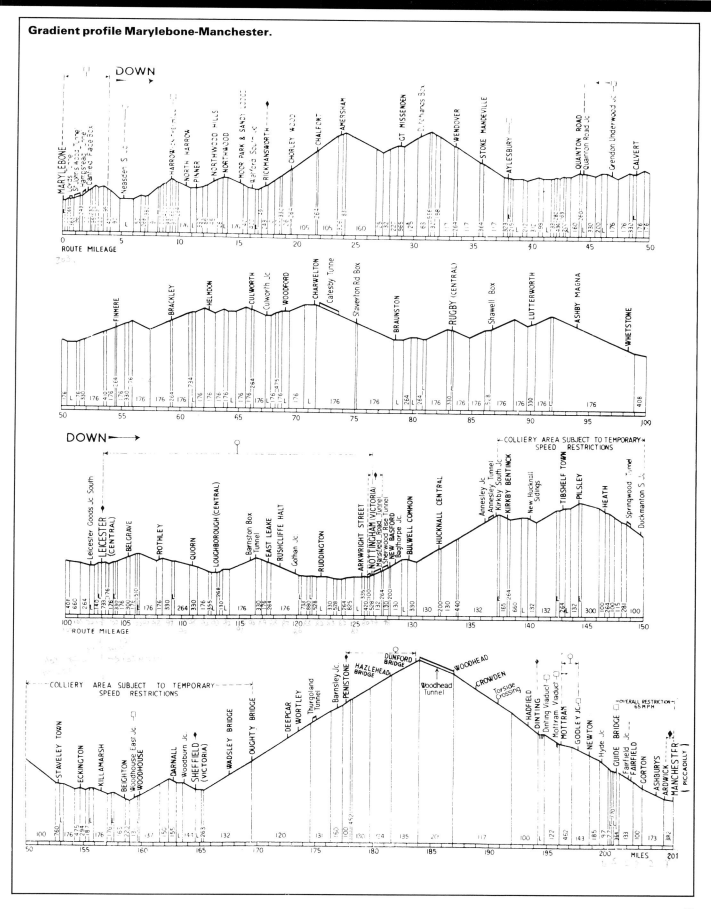

Gradient profile Marylebone-Manchester.

51

At Wembley Park we sweep past a locomotive-hauled electric on the 'Met', headed by *Dick Whittington*. The driver glances at the gauges, and sees the steam gauge is steady with the needle almost 'glued' to the red mark. *Kudu* is recently ex-works, and everything is going swimmingly. Shortly before Harrow, we again cross the LNWR line for the second of the three times this will occur on our journey north. The driver now eases down the regulator and lets the rising gradient gradually bring down our speed for the 40-50mph speed restrictions through the stations at Harrow-on-the-Hill and North Harrow. If judged correctly, this will save applying the brakes. Once clear of Harrow, the gradient eases out, and *Kudu* is opened out once more. The fireman is again busy on the shovel meeting his driver's demands on the boiler. Our speed is now rising rapidly and, after we pass the bright and clean Metropolitan station of Moor Park, the driver puts on the jet (or blower to Midland men) and shuts the regulator. The brakes are now applied fiercely, as before us looms Rickmansworth station with its severe 25mph speed restriction round its curves. The idea is to bring the train speed down early and make sure the brakes are fully released, as we clear the station. The train now faces the climb over the Chilterns and we don't want dragging brakes to impede us.

The harsh bark of the 'B1', now heard rebounding from the deep sides of the chalk cutting, is punctuated by the metallic ring of the shovel as the fireman keeps up a practised swing from the tender plate into the small opening on the firebox door known to GC men as 'the trap'. Having passed the stations at Chorleywood and Chalfont, where the Chesham branch forks off, we are now approaching the top of our climb at Amersham. Even if blindfolded, the crew would know their whereabouts by the beautiful scent emanating from the perfume factory on the up side. Once through the station our speed builds up quickly and the driver notches up the cut-off to about 20%. After checking his fire the fireman now looks out for the Great Missenden distant signal, as the curvature of the line means he will see it fractionally before the driver. When you are travelling at slightly more than the line maximum speed, every second counts!

'It's on here mate', shouts the fireman as he sights the distant at 'caution', at the same time hanging on the whistle to send a reminder to the 'bobby'. In a flash the driver has shut off steam and opened the jet in one combined movement. There is the sound of in-rushing air as he makes a typical GC brake application, bringing the train pipe needle on the vacuum gauge down to zero. The smell of hot metal permeates the cab as the brakes begin to bite, and our speed is soon under control. The home signal stays resolutely 'on' until we have stopped, whereupon the signalman eases it 'off' slowly and then holds a red flag out, meaning we are to draw up and stop at the box. The signalman then instructs us to proceed with caution as there are sheep on the line before Wendover. We carry on and, shortly after passing the starting signal, we see a red-faced farmer repairing the fence and a ganger waving that everything is now OK.

The driver now really 'gives her the gun' as there is still a fair climb out of the Great Missenden dip, and we are now a few minutes behind time. We blast on over the summit and tear down the grade through Wendover, setting some loose papers on the platform swirling up like a miniature whirlwind. Approaching Stoke Mandeville the driver shuts off steam again, as just north of the station is another speed restriction of 40mph owing to a slip in the bank. Just a slight rubbing of the brake and we are off again.

As we pass through Aylesbury, the driver looks at his watch and gestures to his mate with three fingers pointing at the floor, meaning the train is three minutes down. The fireman has to busy himself with the 'dustpan' now as he knows his mate will try to recover the time, and the section ahead is one of the hardest on the route. On we forge — past the lonely station at Quainton Road, over the points at Grendon Underwood Junction and past the acrid-smelling chimneys of Calvert brickworks. The line is now of an undulating nature with climbs and dips all the way to Woodford. Just as the crew think they are doing well, the Culworth Junction distant is now seen to be 'on'. Once again we hear the piercing scream of the 'B1s' whistle as the driver shuts his regulator and brakes fiercely. As we are approaching the home signal it suddenly swings up as does the starter as well. We also notice that the colour light distant for Woodford No 4 signalbox also changes from yellow to green. Possibly the signalman has let a freight train off the Banbury branch and it has taken a fraction too long getting into the goods road at No 4. Once again No 61008 has to be opened out and, as we roar through Woodford station, we spot a freight train with an 'Austerity' 2-8-0 at the head clanking up the goods road towards No 2 signalbox. The driver whistles the time-honoured 'long and a short' to the crew of the 'Austerity' and holds up two fingers to signify he has caused us to lose two minutes. The Woodford man returns a two-finger salute which has a slightly different message!

After clearing Woodford and its yards, the fireman now has another duty to perform which mustn't be missed. Ahead lie Charwelton troughs and the supply in our 4,200gal tank is getting rather low. The fireman whirls the scoop handle round furiously and then opens the 'telltale' to watch the water seep from the holes in the rod as it rises in the tank. With good judgement, the scoop will be raised before allowing the tank to overflow. Once through Charwelton station we plunge into the dark of Catesby tunnel. Although dead straight for its 3,000yd, one rarely sees through it, as the 'runners' pounding up the bank keep it pretty well filled with smoke. The fireman keeps well forward in the cab, as 200yd inside the tunnel is a very bad piece of track which can given you a nasty bump if you are caught unawares on the lap plate between the engine and the tender.

Steam is now shut off again and we can freewheel down the grade through Staverton Road and Braunstone & Willoughby. We burst into the daylight from the north portal, our front windows covered in huge black blobs of sooty water from the tunnel roof. Immediately to the north of the tunnel is a small overbridge reputed to be of very tight clearance. In fact, on the up side of the arch, the chips knocked out of the bricks by fire irons can still be seen to this day.

As we run into Rugby we are still a couple of minutes down, but smart work by the station staff sees us away just a minute late. This means we now have to run the 20 miles to Leicester in 22min. The engine is thrashed away from Rugby to get her swinging through the dip to attack Shawell bank. As we blast over the girder bridge, we again cross the LNWR main line for the third time since leaving Marylebone.

During the assault on Shawell the fireman takes the bent dart out of the fire iron cubicle and pokes the fire from the back of the firebox. This is the last chance to get rid of any excess fire up the chimney. The shed disposal men don't take too kindly to arriving on shed with a firebox full of unnecessary fire. The engine breasts Shawell summit going like a bat out of hell and flies down through Lutterworth station, whistling a warning to the few passengers waiting for the up 'ord'. After breasting the top of the short rise that follows, the hard work for this crew is nearly over.

Our speed increases rapidly now as we dive into Ashby tunnel (note — *never* called Dunton Basset tunnel by any railwaymen), and through the station. The driver pulls out his watch and, seeing that he now has 9min to reach Leicester, shuts his regulator and gives a thumbs up sign to his mate. The fireman has put on the live steam injector and slacks down the ever present coal dust on the footplate. Even shut off, our speed is now well over 80mph as we fly down the bank towards Whetstone. As we start to lean towards the right, the fireman sights Whetstone's distant and shouts out 'Right away mate'. As we shoot through the station, the fireman acknowledges the waves from his Leicester mates who are waiting in the loop with the returning pick-up from Lutterworth. The driver now cracks open his regulator to keep up the momentum as the track levels out slightly at Aylestone. As we approach Leicester South Goods signalbox the approach-lit signal gives a green aspect and the driver now shuts off for the final time. We trot past the locomotive shed and yards and, as we pass the carriage sheds, the driver commences his braking. We clatter through the girder bridge and over the viaduct, diving into the platform at a little over the permitted 25mph and screech to a halt outside the gents. The fireman jumps off to place one of the headlamps on the tender end, while the driver winds the engine into back gear to 'ease up' for the shunter to uncouple (note that railwaymen never used the term 'reverse' — it was always 'back gear').

Waiting alongside is Leicester 'V2' No 60879 which will take the train on to Sheffield Victoria. Our driver informs his opposite number of the train's load, and the 'B1' and her crew now repair to the shed, their day's work done. The driver feels pleased with his efforts as he recovered the lost time. Sadly, he is destined not to be driving on the main line for much longer. When leaving London one day on the 12.15 down, he will be tragically hit in the eye by an air gun pellet fired from the flats at Canfield Place, and will finish his time until retirement ignominiously driving a broom round the shed floor.

The 'V2' now backs on to the train and couples up. We are away on time and there is a new urgency about the sound of the engine. Instead of the sharp crack of the 'B1', we are now treated to the syncopated three-cylinder beat, as 60879 strides out past the petrol tanks at Abbey Lane and up to Belgrave & Birstall station. Once over the top the driver 'screws her neck' and we are simply flying down through Rothley, Swithland with its reservoir, and Quorn.

Now the driver shuts off steam and we commence braking for the Loughborough stop. We arrive in the platform having taken a little over 10min from Leicester. The train is away on time and once again some heavy climbing is before us until we reach the top of the bank at the short tunnel at Barnstone. Now the driver can notch the cut-off right up to 15% and the 'Green Arrow' really flies down through East Leake, Rushcliffe, Gotham and Ruddington. After Ruddington we pass the long-closed signalbox at Wilford Brick Sidings which still appears to be in good condition. We next dive over the Trent via the steel girder bridge and the driver again shuts off and brakes fiercely for the Arkwright Street curves. We clatter over the bridges carrying us above the rival Midland line and over Weekday Cross Junction where the Great Northern line from Colwick trails in. Through the short tunnel, and we are in to 'the Vic' at Nottingham. The clock is showing 6.15pm, so we are on time. The firemen busies himself, filling up the back corners of the firebox ready for

Right:

The 10.00 down to Manchester is seen between Amersham and Great Missenden with 'A3' 4-6-2 No 60063 *Isinglass* at the head in May 1956.
G. C. Farnell

the stiff climb ahead. Two minutes later at 6.17pm we pull out of the platform and plunge into the smoke-filled gloom of Mansfield Road tunnel. The 'V2' loses her feet momentarily, but a touch of the steam sanders, and she settles down to the regular three-cylinder beat.

The fireman is busy now keeping the back corners topped up. Apart from the short dip through Bulwell Common, it is now all 'against the collar' until we reach Annesley tunnel. After Mansfield Road tunnel comes a short break for the closed Carrington station, after which we head immediately into Sherwood Rise tunnel. Next comes New Basford with its carriage sheds, Bagthorpe Junction where the line to Derby GN forks off and Bulwell Common. Still we climb up and up, the fireman feeds his fire with a steady rhythm. These short square fireboxes are well liked by GC men because if you keep the back corners filled up, not a lot of effort is required to keep rolling the coal inside the firehole door.

We pass Annesley with its huge yards and evil-smelling slag heaps behind the locomotive shed. Once through the tunnel we can ease off, as the myriad of speed restrictions between here and Sheffield means we are continually either shutting off and braking, or thrashing the engine between the restrictions. Our progress is still upwards as the 'V2' pounds up through Tibshelf and Pilsley stations until we reach the top of the bank. Now the speed really increases as we fly down through Heath station and junction where the line diverges for Chesterfield. Next comes Springwood tunnel where the driver eases open the regulator. This is a precaution as with a 'V2' the clearance between chimney top and tunnel roof is a bit tight and, if you are running with

steam shut off, it is not unusual to get a bad blow-back of flames through the firehole door. As we emerge, the driver shuts off again and we rock through Duckmanton Junction and charge on down the bank.

As Staveley's distant signal comes into view, the brakes are again brought into action as yet another speed restriction is in force through Staveley station. The collieries have a lot to answer for in this neck of the woods. More restrictions apply through Renishaw and over the now permanently dry troughs at Killamarsh. Next comes a real rarity — the only level crossing on the main line between Sheffield and London, at Beighton. The driver opens up again as we climb up through Woodhouse Junction, where the line from Retford joins us, and start bearing westward.

Now comes a new feature of the GC; the overhead electric wires start at Rotherwood and will accompany us for the rest of our journey. As we forge on up the heat from the coke ovens can be felt as we pass Orgreave coke works box. Shortly after this, we are over the summit and can shut off as we run through Darnall with its well-lit engine shed, Woodburn Junction, and so into Sheffield Victoria station at 7.15pm (right time).

Before the advent of the Manchester-Sheffield electrification, our crew would now be faced with the climb over the Pennines to Manchester. As it is, they will now uncouple to make way for the 'Juice Jack' to carry the train forward. As the 'V2' is too long to be accommodated on the Sheffield turntable, it now runs light to Darnall shed and the crew face a fairly lengthy wait until they work back with the 'London Mail' at midnight.

Left:
'A3' No 60104 *Solario* storms along between Amersham and Great Missenden with the up 'Master Cutler' in May 1956. *G. C. Farnell*

Below:
Before the two extra lines were built between Rickmansworth and Harrow, 'A3' Pacific No 60050 *Persimmon* makes a delightful picture on the 'Master Cutler' for Marylebone travelling between Northwood Hills and Pinner in April 1955. *G. C. Farnell*

Top:
'V2' 2-6-2 No 60879 climbs with superb exhaust through the Chilterns with the 06.20 from Nottingham (07.20 from Leicester Central) stopper to London Marylebone on a glorious day in 1957.
G. C. Farnell

Above right:
Leicester's Len Woodhead, with local 'V2' 2-6-2 No 60878, brings the down 'South Yorkshireman' towards Rugby Central on 26 May 1958. *M. Mensing*

Right:
'A3' Pacific No 60049 *Galtee More* tears through Woodford with the 15.20 Marylebone-Manchester on 2 August 1952.
P. H. Wells

Top:
'A3' Pacific No 60044 *Melton* eases round the curves at Harrow-on-the-Hill with the 15.20 Marylebone-Manchester in March 1957. *G. C. Farnell*

Above left:
The up 'South Yorkshireman' runs past the island platform at Woodford Halse headed by 'B1' 4-6-0 No 61106 on 29 May 1959. *S. Creer*

Left:
The up 'South Yorkshireman' strides away from Sheffield Victoria in the hands of Leicester 'Black Five' No 45186 on 4 October 1958. The 'C13' 4-4-2T is on station pilot duty.
K. R. Pirt

Top:
At Marylebone, 'K3' 2-6-0 No 61853 has been turned and moves to take water prior to working the 12.15 to Manchester as far as Leicester in February 1959. Although not normal express power, the 'K3s' were no slouches in the right hands and would usually achieve a 'right time' arrival. *G. C. Farnell*

Right:
Driver Sid Lees looks back for the guard's signal, whilst Fireman Arthur Jones prepares to shovel, when waiting to leave Aylesbury Town with the up 'South Yorkshireman', due in Marylebone at 15.29 in November 1958. 'V2' No 60879 is the capable locomotive. *G. C. Farnell*

Left:
The 10.00 Marylebone-Manchester (London Road) waits to leave Aylesbury behind 'V2' No 60876 in April 1958. The 'V2s' were ideal for the GC section expresses, their smaller wheels providing greater pulling power and enabling faster acceleration than the Pacifics. *G. C. Farnell*

Top right:
'A3' Pacific No 60107 *Royal Lancer* stands at Marylebone with the 'Master Cutler' (18.18 to Sheffield) on 11 July 1953. Note the station signalbox, long since demolished, and the relative calm of the preparation for departure. *J. F. Henton*

Centre right:
The up 'Master Cutler' leaves Nottingham on 2 March 1949 with 'A3' No 60054 *Prince of Wales* in charge. The train is running off the Nottingham blue brick viaducts past Queens Walk yards, towards the Trent Bridge. Note the original headboard, an example of which can be seen today in the National Railway Museum. *J. F. Henton*

Bottom right:
'B1' 4-6-0 No 61159, with white discs rather than headlamps, accelerates away from Nottingham Victoria and over Weekday Cross Junction (where the Grantham line forks off) with the up 'South Yorkshireman' on 10 May 1949. *J. F. Henton*

6

Fast Freight and Parcels

Leicester Central shed did not feature as prominently in the GC freight operations as it did in passenger services. The main GC freight flow from Annesley to Woodford ran through Leicester, and Annesley also despatched through fitted freights to the West and London, usually from York. Locomotives would work through from the North and reach Leicester, Woodford or Banbury. Motive power normally consisted of 'V2s', 'K3s' and 'B16s'. 'B1s' worked through as well, and the GC fish trains were hauled by 'K3s' and later Immingham 'Britannias'. Leicester crews did at least operate these fish trains. Parcels services were numerous too. Daytime services consisted of the Banbury-York and the Nottingham-Marylebone vans. During the evening, along with the 'Newspaper', there were services to and from Manchester and to Preston. Freight services were either rerouted or withdrawn by June 1965, except for the 11.15 Nottingham-Marylebone parcels which ran right up to the final day.

Frank Stratford

As stated previously, Leicester Central men did not figure very prominently in the main line freight business, as the depot was mainly responsible for passenger workings. The bulk of the freight trains were run in the main by Annesley men on the well known 'Windcutter' service, Woodford shed handling many of the fitted freights. Before the Annesley-Woodford service commenced, Leicester men had relieved and worked a lot of southbound coal trains, especially in the 'Control Link' on which men signed on duty and waited for instructions from control as to which trains to work.

In my time at Leicester Central, we only worked a few freight trains. These were the Lutterworth pick-up, the

Thompson 'O1' 2-8-0 No 63890 enters Nottingham Victoria on an Annesley-Woodford freight before these services were almost exclusively handed over to '9F' 2-10-0s. The date is September 1955. *J. F. Henton*

Loughborough pick-up and the Abbey Lane petrol shunt. There was also a midday train which went to the Ministry of Defence sidings at Ruddington and on return picked up the gypsum that Colwick men had brought up the Gotham branch and also the same from Hotchley Hill. This train was often very heavily loaded when leaving Hotchley Hill. There was also a night train to Woodford, which cleared the yard at Leicester with all the southbound traffic, with a corresponding Woodford-Leicester working. In the other direction was the 21.10 to Annesley, which usually picked up at Nottingham Goods en route. The return working of this train was a freight which often included a GW pannier tank being hauled from the makers to Swindon and one would also encounter engines making their way home after shopping at Doncaster and Darlington, such as Neasden 'L1s' or 'Westernised' Austerity 2-8-0s.

Driving passenger and freight trains required different techniques. Whereas the skill on the express passenger was running at high speeds and keeping to a strict timetable to ensure that connections were made, the driver of the freight train, although still having a booked timetable to run to, had problems of another kind — especially those involved in keeping control of his train on undulating stretches of line such as the Great Central. A heavy loose-coupled freight must rank among the most difficult of trains to work. On starting, it was a case of slow but sure, tightening each wagon coupling one at a time so as not to wrap the guard around his stove pipe. When the driver shut off steam at the top of a bank the fireman would normally wind on the tender handbrake to keep the wagons buffered up, so that when the driver started to apply the engine brake once again, the guard would not be put through the van window!

When nearing the bottom of a bank, the driver would crack open the regulator as the fireman eased off the tender brake. This would stretch out the couplings, thus ensuring that there would be no snatching as the next uphill gradient was reached. To watch an experienced driver was an education and as a fireman one picked up the various skills from being booked to work with different men. Each one had various little wrinkles of his own and the good fireman would watch, listen and learn for the future.

Working a long fully-fitted freight posed different problems. Although close-coupled and therefore not presenting much of a problem when starting, troubles could occur when braking. If the vacuum brake was applied too fiercely it would take a long time to recreate the vacuum and the brakes could still be dragging at the rear of the train. If a driver accelerated too quickly a violent snatch would result; more than one driver on the Great Central broke his train in half through this happening.

The troubles that could occur were brought home to me nearing the end of my career on BR; I was driving a Class 25 diesel on the Corby-Oldbury freight which had a fitted head of one third of the vehicles being vacuum braked. Just entering the goods line at Water Orton, I inadvertently let my foot off the dead man's pedal. This has the effect of a full emergency brake application and, with the front third of the train stopping dead suddenly, the unbraked rear portion buffers up suddenly, and when the shock waves reach the guard's van it can result in chaos. I sent my mate back to check the train and guard were OK, as this was part of the regulations, and when he enquired if the guard was alright, the reply was 'Yes, I heard it coming and baled out in time'. He swore that the brake van jumped a foot in the air!

Above right:
An up fish train is seen crossing the River Trent at Nottingham Goods South, with 'K3' 2-6-0 No 61845 in charge on 28 July 1951.
J. F. Henton

Right:
York 'V2' No 60961 storms through Rugby with the 'Cardiff' fitted freight on 27 February 1965. The engine worked as far as Woodford Halse; the train came from Tees yard.
D. Smith

The best known of the long-distance fitted freights on the GC were the various fish trains that originated from Hull and Grimsby and ran to such places as Cardiff, Whitland and Swindon. One train from Grimsby in the afternoon was an Immingham 'K3' turn in Eastern Region days. The engine would run through to Banbury and would never be worked by Leicester men. However, in later years when the 'Britannias' showed up on the job, it was worked by Leicester shed for a short time. Again for a short period the same train was routed via Calvert where it then reversed on to the Bletchley to Oxford line and was worked by Leicester men as far as Oxford.

Another afternoon train used to arrive in Leicester in the charge of a Doncaster 'B1' 4-6-0 which later returned to its home with the Marylebone (Goods) to Doncaster parcels. This train was worked forward by either Leicester or Banbury men, who returned home after working the Bournemouth-York to Leicester. Nobody could understand why the diagram office would change the jobs round. For a period Leicester men would work the fish to Banbury whilst Banbury men returned on the 17.22 local. Then after a while the jobs would be reversed with Banbury men taking the fish and Leicester men the passenger.

A long-standing Leicester turn was the Swindon fish train which left Leicester in the early hours of the morning. Originally there had been two trains with the two engines returning light coupled together. With the rationalisation that took place, these were later worked as only one train from Leicester. The two separate trains arrived in Leicester and were then shunted by the station pilot to make up one train. The train detached vans at Banbury, Oxford and Marston sidings and these would be marshalled outside the brake van. After arrival at Swindon we would uncouple and, as we did not need coal, we would not need to go on Swindon shed, but would turn on the 'Factory' turntable and return light engine. This was a mileage turn for Leicester, so we were always in a hurry as it was no use making overtime on a mileage job; if we went to Swindon and back in 8hr, we would be paid for 14hr, for there was 6hr's mileage pay allowed for the turn. If the trip took us 14hr, that is what we would be paid for.

To facilitate a quick return, Leicester men used to get up to a few ruses, one of which was to 'lash up' the Swindon signalmen with white rags. These hand cloths were akin to the ordinary dish cloth, but were much sought after by GW men who were only issued with cotton waste as a hand cleaner. Very often, we would be running through the middle road at Swindon station while the Cardiff-Paddington sleeper stood in the platform. To see the crew's faces as we shot through with a light engine only 5min before their departure time was a joy to behold. The idea was to get round Didcot Junction as quickly as possible, when we could be clear of the sleeper. If we ever checked it, the signalman would not let us precede it the following morning. We therefore used to really 'go for it' and it was not unusual to run the 20 miles to Didcot in something like 17min! Western men thought we were mad to run at such speeds on a light engine with no GW automatic train control fitted. Alas, one day they were proved right. Leicester Driver Ken Davis misread the signals on a very misty morning when he was unusually routed on to the slow line and ran out of road at Knighton Crossing signalbox, burying a 'B1' up to the top framing in the sand drag.

A very amusing incident happened at Oxford one night when I was on this turn with Driver Jack Wright. We had pulled into the middle road to wait for the station pilot to detach the vans from our rear. In the platform was a 'Castle' on a parcels train. At this time, Saltley men were working as far as Banbury, and the Western man mistook us for one of them, as we were on one of the then newly-arrived 'Black Fives'. Looking us over, he said to Jack 'Are you bloody Saltley men getting as far as Oxford now then?' to which Jack laconically replied, referring to the GW automatic train control, 'Put me one of them ting-a-lings on mate, and I'll go through to Newton Abbot!'

We also had a nice little arrangement whereby the signalman at Heyford always had his kettle boiling for us on our return trip, and we would keep his bunker topped up with coal from the tender. I always enjoyed my turns on the Swindon fish but when we had engines such as the Standard '4' 4-6-0s, we often ran into trouble when returning light engine as some of the signalmen, on hearing our Western-like whistles, would try and route us on to the shed at places such as Oxford and Banbury, thinking we were GW men. This was possibly because the day shift would be on duty by the time we arrived back at Oxford and perhaps would not realise who we were.

One well known Leicester turn was the famous 'Newspaper' from Marylebone to Nottingham. Leicester men worked up to London with the last express of the day from Manchester and had quite a long wait before working back with the newspaper train in the early hours. The railway company originally had to get special permission, with the blessing of the trade union, to roster the men on a 10hr duty. The train was originally routed over the normal 'Met' route via Aylesbury, but at some times, especially on Monday mornings, it would be diverted over the GW/GC Joint line via High Wycombe. It was worked throughout from Marylebone to Nottingham by Leicester depot until the final years, after which Neasden men worked the train to Woodford, where a special stop for relief was inserted for the Leicester men to take over. Even later still, in the latter years of the GC, Cricklewood men worked the train to Leicester, with a Type 2 diesel and returned to London light engine. Not a bad job for a fireman, when one thinks back to the sweat lost in former years, on 'B1s', 'A3s' and 'V2s'. The 'V2' was possibly the best engine on the job; with its 6ft 2in wheels it was a good hill climber and would also 'fly' down the dips. The load was always 10 vehicles making 340 tons but was much heavier than this when the weight of all the newspapers was added. There was also one passenger coach included in the formation, as the train was advertised in the public timetable. If ever there was a train you could set your clock by, it was the 'Papers' and very rarely would we be late arriving in Leicester unless the cause was something beyond the control of the enginemen. Talking about Leicester 'V2s' reminds me of a terrible mishap that occurred with one, on another of Leicester's fitted train turns, the 20.45 Marylebone (Goods)-Doncaster parcels. We used to work up to Marylebone with the 14.10 from Manchester and return with this train. In fact, at one time the up train used to run double-headed, the second engine returning with the 20.50 Preston parcels — a train diverted from the LNWR main line during its electrification.

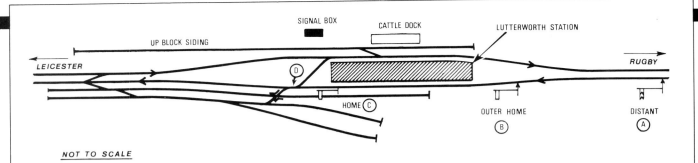

Lutterworth station — location of the accident described by the Author. (A) is the down distant signal which was missed by the crew of 'V2' No 60854. In spite of a full brake application, the train continued past the outer home (B) and home (C) signals and collided with the up freight train at point (D).

On the night in question — it was during Christmas 1957 — I was on this turn with Driver Ted Rodwell. Our engine was 'V2' No 60854 — a real 'good 'un' which was shedded at Leicester for a short time. We had had no worries on the up journey, the engine having been well in command of the job. Things were also going swimmingly on the parcels, until we were almost on Leicester's 'doorstep' when a chain of circumstances lured us into a horrible collision at Lutterworth. Firstly, I will try to explain the lead-up to it. When on a familiar working drivers would obviously notice certain trains running in the opposite direction. If both trains were on time, we would pass at roughly the same place on each occasion. An up train we usually met at Rugby was the Sheffield-Swindon, still known to all and sundry as the 'Penzance'. On the day in question, we were well past Rugby, having climbed the bank at Shawell, and were approaching Lutterworth when we met the 'Penzance' roaring southwards with sparks flying skywards from the chimney. Thinking we might be running out of course, Ted, whose timepiece had been acting up, drew the recalcitrant pocket watch from his overalls and asked me what time my watch was showing. In that fatal second, as we bent down to compare our watches in the light from the firebox door, we had unwittingly run past the Lutterworth distant, which was showing 'caution'. The curvature of the line at this point was to the right and as I got up I saw the red light of the outer home signal. 'It's on here' I shouted to Ted, who immediately shut off steam and made a full brake application. Alas, we only had a very short train on this occasion and, although we were not going too fast, we were not stopping very quickly either. We slid past both the outer home and the home signal, and just past this, with our speed down to almost 10mph, we struck an up 'runner' which had been shunted

across the road. It transpired that the signalman had attempted to back the 'runner' into his up block siding but found that it was too long, so he then had to back it across the road on to the down main line to let the impatient 'Penzance' by. The 'runner' was just pulling forward again over the cross-over to follow the passenger train when we collided with it — our buffers coming between the third and fourth wagons. Although we had almost stopped by then, the Annesley driver had pulled his wagons all over the railway before he could bring his train to a stand. The front part of his train consisted of box vans full of aluminium ingots which were strewn around everywhere. In effect, our 'V2' was not even off the road, and when the Woodford breakdown train came behind us, they immediately drew our train and engine clear of the wreckage.

Even in disaster there is sometimes humour. The regulations in force ruled that I was now obliged to repair to the signalbox to carry out Rule 55, which every fireman had to do if his train was standing at signals for more than the prescribed time. I had picked my way through a panorama of splintered wagons and ingots that looked like a battlefield and as I entered the box the signalman, who was prone to stutter, implied that we were to blame and not him with the immortal statement 'Y-Y-You've run by my boards'!

In such cases as ours, a driver would often be demoted to the shed link after an enquiry. In Ted Rodwell's case, he kept his link position having received a reprimand at Derby. A short time before the accident Ted's wife had passed away and he was left to bring up two sons. His family circumstances were obviously looked upon sympathetically and taken into account by the line manager. As stated before, the incident earned Ted the nickname of 'Mister Magoo'.

Right:
A Woodford-York fitted freight is seen passing New Basford powered by York 'V2' No 60805 on 10 June 1963. The carriage sidings can be seen to the left of the locomotive.
T. Boustead

LOCOMOTIVE ALLOCATIONS – ANNESLEY MPD

Date: Winter 1955
Region: Eastern
Shed Code: 38B

61063	63579	63610	63670	63740	63784	63806	63867	63890	64370	68976
61066	63589	63619	63676	63746	63786	63808	63868	63901	64406	69651
61209	63590	63630	63678	63752	63789	63817	63869	64292	64431	69692
61975	63591	63646	63687	63768	63792	63838	63872	64300	67363	
61980	63592	63650	63689	63773	63795	63854	63879	64318	68896	
63571	63594	63652	63711	63777	63796	63863	63886	64354	68927	
63578	63596	63663	63725	63780	63803	63865	63887	64361	68975	

Date: Summer 1959
Region: London Midland
Shed Code: 16D

42339	61856	63610	63777	63838	63901	64747	92014	92067	92073	92088	92095
42769	61975	63676	63792	63854	64359	64798	92030	92068	92074	92089	92096
42784	61980	63689	63796	63865	64375	92010	92031	92069	92075	92090	
42847	63578	63711	63806	63867	64420	92011	92032	92070	92076	92091	
42872	63579	63740	63808	63869	64439	92012	92033	92071	92081	92092	
42897	63591	63752	63817	63886	64739	92013	92043	92072	92087	92093	

Date: January 1963
Region: London Midland
Shed Code: 16D

44665	46101	*Royal Scots Grey*	46163	*Civil Service Rifleman*	48002	48099
44717	46111	*Royal Fusilier*	46169	*The Boy Scout*	48007	48117
45215	46112	*Sherwood Forester*			48011	48141
45217	46122	*Royal Ulster Rifleman*			48024	48142
45234	46126	*Royal Army Service Corps*			48057	48168
45267	46143	*South Staffordshire Regiment*			48064	48293
45450	46158	*The Loyal Regiment*			48079	48304

48324	84006	92012	93033	92069	92075	92090	92095
48333	84007	92013	92043	92071	92076	92091	92096
48378	84027	92014	92057	92072	92087	92092	
48165	92010	92030	92067	92073	92088	92093	
48770	92011	92032	92068	92074	92089	92094	

Left:
'Royal Scot' 4-6-0 No 46156 *The South Wales Borderer* is seen drifting down the bank from Tibshelf to New Hucknall with an up coke train on 25 October 1963.
J. S. Hancock

LOCOMOTIVE ALLOCATIONS – WOODFORD HALSE MPD

Date: Winter 1955-56
Region: Eastern
Shed Code: 38E

60817	60890	61368	64331	64428	90040	90095	90365	90484	90509	90638	13066
60831	60915	64324	64364	69069	90046	90137	90403	90486	90516	90672	13067
60871	61078	64327	64388	90033	90065	90218	90448	90504	90520	90697	13068
60879	61192	64330	64418	90039	90080	90299	90474	90507	90574		13069

Date: Summer 1959
Region: London Midland
Shed Code: 2F

43063	60815	61368	61843	90033	90137	90433	90520	D3066
43106	60890	61804	61853	90040	90218	90448	90574	D3067
43330	60915	61809	65158	90046	90237	90474	90638	D3068
43389	61078	61824	67740	90065	90299	90486	90672	D3069
43394	61186	61838	67771	90066	90346	90504	90697	
	61192	61841	67789	90080	90365	90507		
	61271	61842		90095	90403	90516		

Date: January 1963
Region: London Midland
Shed Code: 2F

42157	44846		73032	90033	90365	90563	D3066
42178	45285		73045	90040	90433	90589	D3067
42250	48385		73053	90065	90448	90672	D3068
42251	48386		73066	90066	90474	90697	D3069
42252	48650		73159	90095	90486		
42253	61008 *Kudu*		76044	90218	90504		
42281	61116		76052	90237	90516		
44667	73000		76087	90299	90520		
44688	73010			90346	90524		
44691							

Below:
Petrol tanks for Abbey Lane sidings are whisked through Rugby by BR '9F' 2-10-0 No 92091 on 17 November 1964.
P. H. Wells

Top:
An up 'runner' storms through the 'Birdcage' bridge over the West Coast main line at Rugby with BR '9F' 2-10-0 No 92090 well in charge on 17 October 1964. *P. H. Wells*

Right:
Sunday working. '9F' 2-10-0 No 92093 approaches Rugby Central with an up load of steel bars on 11 September 1960. *M. Mensing*

Below right:
Thompson 'O1' 2-8-0 No 63784 heads an up coal train through Tibshelf on 9 May 1963. Coal was a major component of GC freight traffic, the Nottinghamshire collieries feeding into the GC main line at Annesley yard, from which the product was then moved swiftly to the south. *J. F. Henton*

Left:
'Black Five' 4-6-0 No 44863 passes New Basford on 8 June 1963 with a down fitted freight. Sherwood Rise tunnel is in the background.
T. Boustead

Below left:
Under a seasonal covering of snow on 28 December 1964, York's 'V2' No 60847 *St Peter's School York AD627*, with the middle cylinder piston gland blowing badly, heads an up fitted freight towards Belgrave & Birstall. *J. H. Cooper-Smith*

Bottom:
WD 'Austerity' 2-8-0 No 90337 blows off as she waits for the signals to clear for the Stratford & Midland Junction line at Woodford Halse in September 1961.
G. C. Farnell

Above:
A York-Woodford 'fitted' is seen from a road bridge near Charwelton headed by 'V2' No 60886 on 13 February 1965. The loops and sidings had by now been lifted as the process of run-down took hold. *G. T. Robinson*

Left:
An up freight for Annesley yard approaches Annesley tunnel with 'B1' 4-6-0 No 61098 in control on 27 February 1960. *J. Cupit*

Left:
**Double-chimney 'V2'
No 60963 enters Rugby
Central with the 11.15
Nottingham Victoria-
Neasden empty vans in
May 1964.** *R. P. Hendry*

Below:
**WD 'Austerity' 2-8-0
No 90520 clanks through
Aylesbury with an up
mixed freight for Neasden
in November 1957.**
G. C. Farnell

Left:
**Woodford's 'J39' 0-6-0
No 64809 is pictured on
the Woodford pick-up
freight in the up loop at
Rugby Central as a
passenger train passes in
September 1961.**
G. C. Farnell

Top:
Woodford 'Austerity' 2-8-0 No 90520 heads north from Princes Risborough en route to its home depot with coal empties from Neasden yard in July 1957. *G. C. Farnell*

Above right:
'Black Five' 4-6-0 No 44830 makes for Ashendon Junction and approaches the one-time Ilmer Halt with empty vans for Sheffield in July 1960. *G. C. Farnell*

Right:
The up empty vans for Neasden enter Woodford station with BR Standard '5' 4-6-0 No 73032 in charge in April 1961.
G. C. Farnell

Top:
GWR '28xx' 2-8-0 No 2857 trundles along the up goods line at Woodford in September 1961. The 'broomsticks' under the smoke box can be clearly seen. *G. C. Farnell*

Left:
Woodford 'Austerity' 2-8-0 No 90237 blasts through the platform with an up freight in September 1961. The signalbox behind the locomotive is Woodford No 3 while the shed coaling plant is visible in the far distance.
G. C. Farnell

Above:
'J39' 0-6-0 No 64727 crosses from the GC main line on to the S&MJ route for Stratford-upon-Avon in September 1961. Noticeable is the short section between Woodford's No 4 and No 3 signalboxes, both of which are visible in the picture.
G. C. Farnell

Left:
WD 'Austerity' 2-8-0 No 90095 heads from Woodford towards Culworth Junction and the Western Region at Banbury in November 1961. The hopper wagons behind the tender are loaded with gypsum being conveyed from Hotchley Hill to Blechington Cement Works. *G. C. Farnell*

Right:
An 'Austerity' 2-8-0 heads into the old down yard at Woodford with an Engineers' train in April 1961. *G. C. Farnell*

Below right:
'B1' 4-6-0 No 61186 heads south from Woodford with Nottingham-Neasden newspaper empties in September 1961.
G. C. Farnell

Bottom:
BR Standard '4' 2-6-0 No 76039 shunts the yards at Woodford after arriving with a freight from Neasden yard in April 1961. *G. C. Farnell*

7

Cross-Country and Special Workings

Frank Stratford

Although the London extension was a simple and straightforward line to work, Leicester men did work away from the GC over other routes. There were not many junctions on the GC compared with its Midland neighbour, where one could be diverted at least eight different ways from Leicester to Birmingham. Our main diversion from the GC line was of course the line from Culworth Junction to Banbury, which opened up the way to the west.

The long standing turn at Leicester was the York-Bournemouth passenger service, which was worked by a Leicester engine and crew to Banbury. After arrival, we would repair to the shed to turn and get water. The turntable at Banbury was a typical Great Western push-round affair. They must have had some strong arms on the GWR!

It wasn't too bad with a 'B1' as one could usually get it balanced easily enough, but get a 'V2' and it could be trouble, as Ron Smith and I discovered one day with No 60863. We were struggling to keep the turntable on the move, and halfway round we ground to a halt. Ron asked me to move the engine back a little while he checked the balance of the turntable. As anyone who has worked on 'V2s' will know, the brakes were very poor and also slow to react when running light engine. Unfortunately, I couldn't stop in time and the trailing tender wheels dropped off the end of the turntable deck. Nobody seemed to have noticed and we decided to try and jump them on again. This time Ron was in the chair and, as I had done, he was also unable to control the brake. The tender wheels jumped on alright, but we promptly put the front pony wheels off at the other end! This time our plight was seen by the Shed Foreman and within seconds we were swamped with people offering all kinds of advice. Anyway, we were eventually rerailed, and able to

continue on our way. After departing the shed, our next job was the two-coach 'motor' to Woodford which was stabled in the bay. On our way, we stopped at the small halts at Chalcombe Road and Eydon Road. In the days of the '9Fs' the engine was almost longer than the train!

Having arrived at Woodford, we stabled the two coaches, picked up a three-coach set, and worked back to Banbury with another local, where we ran round our train and, after the 'Castle'-hauled 'Inter City' had roared through at a breathtaking speed which must have been near to 40mph, we left with the well loaded commuter service to Woodford. We ran into the 'wooden' platform (concrete actually, but on the railway, names die hard). Here we stood until our Leicester mates had stormed through at something more like express speed with the down 'South Yorkshireman', and then we followed them 'all stations' to Leicester to complete our day. In the summer time we also worked a Saturdays only Newcastle-Bournemouth service on which we worked through to Oxford where a Southern Region engine took over. After a visit to the shed to turn and take on water, we worked a corresponding return train to Leicester.

Other inter-regional trains worked by Leicester men were the Swindon-Sheffield which ran from Monday to Saturday and the Sundays only Sheffield-Swindon and return. The weekday train was a return working after working the 17.22 Leicester-Woodford local, and another local to Banbury. It was always known to GC men as the down 'Penzance' — another old name that refused to die. We left Banbury at 21.18 and, due to the Great Western peculiarity of running with 29in of vacuum when all other regions operated on 21in, it was the job of the shunters to 'pull the strings' on all the coaching stock to make sure that the brakes were fully released before we coupled up to the train. If the job was not

L76/R(HD)

WHITSUNTIDE HOLIDAYS : : 1962

CHEAP TRIP

TO

CLEETHORPES

SUNDAY 10th JUNE 1962

FROM	TIMES OF DEPARTURE	RETURN FARES Second Class	ARRIVAL TIMES ON RETURN
	am	s d	pm
RUGBY Central	9 22	21/–	11 40
LUTTERWORTH	9 34	18/9	11 28
WHETSTONE	9 48	17/3	11 12
LEICESTER Central ...	10 2	17/–	10 59
BELGRAVE & BIRSTALL ...	10 7	16/9	10 52
LOUGHBOROUGH Central ...	10 20	15/9	10 38
EAST LEAKE	10 29	15/–	10 28
RUSHCLIFFE HALT	10 33	15/–	10 22
RUDDINGTON	10 41	15/–	10 14
	pm	Passengers return same day at ...	pm
CLEETHORPES ... arrive	1 47		7 21

CHILDREN under three years of age, free; three years and under fourteen, half-fares (fractions of 1d. reckoned as 1d.).

TICKETS CAN BE OBTAINED IN ADVANCE AT STATIONS AND OFFICIAL RAILWAY AGENTS

Further information will be supplied on application to Stations, Official Railway Agents, or to Mr. L. A. METCALF, District Commercial Manager, LEICESTER. Telephone : Leicester 23841, Extn. 34 ; or Mr. H. BULLOUGH, District Commercial Manager, DERBY. Telephone : Derby 42442, Extn, 204. or Mr. A. S. MEAD, District Passenger Manager, 43 Small Brook, Ringway, BIRMINGHAM. Telephone : Midland 2711.

May, 1962
BR 35000

PX2/Halfex

Arthur Gaunt & Sons (Printers) Ltd., Heanor, Derbyshire.

L90/R(S/Adex)

WHITSUNTIDE HOLIDAYS : : 1962

DAY TRIPS

TO

SKEGNESS

MONDAY 11th JUNE 1962

FROM	TIMES OF DEPARTURE		RETURN FARES Second Class	ARRIVAL TIMES ON RETURN	
Colour of Tickets	**Pink**	**Terra Cotta**	*Colour of Tickets*	**Pink**	**Terra Cotta**
	am	am	s d	pm	am
RUGBY Central	...	8 50	21/–	...	12 42
LUTTERWORTH	...	9 3	18/3	...	12 28
WHETSTONE	...	9 18	17/–	...	12 16
LEICESTER Central	9 12	9 30	16/–	11 43	12 2
					pm
BELGRAVE & BIRSTALL ...	...	9 36˙	16/–	...	11 55
ROTHLEY	...	9 43	16/–	...	11 47
QUORN & WOODHOUSE ...	...	9 50	16/–	...	11 39
LOUGHBOROUGH Central ...	9 27	...	16/–	11 26	...
EAST LEAKE	9 36	...	14/6	11 16	...
RUSHCLIFFE HALT ...	9 40	...	14/6	11 10	...
RUDDINGTON	9 48	...	14/6	11 2	...
ARKWRIGHT STREET... ...	9 55	...	13/6	10 54	...
	pm	pm	Passengers return	pm	pm
SKEGNESS ... ... arrive	12 9	12 27	same day at ...	8 31	8 53

Children under three years of age, free; three years and under fourteen, half-fares, fractions of a 1d. charged as a 1d.

NOTE—LATE BUS ARRANGEMENTS AT LEICESTER
Leicester City Transport will meet the return trains on arrival at Leicester Central Station to convey passengers along the various reouts.
Fares : Adults 1/6d., Children 9d., payable on the buses.

IMPORTANT NOTICE
PASSENGERS MUST TRAVEL, BOTH OUTWARD AND RETURN, BY THE TRAIN CORRESPONDING TO THE COLOUR OF THE RAIL TICKET HELD.
ACCOMMODATION IS LIMITED AND PASSENGERS ARE ADVISED TO BOOK THEIR TICKETS BEFORE THE DAY OF TRAVEL

RAIL TICKETS CAN BE OBTAINED IN ADVANCE AT STATIONS NAMED ONLY

Further information will be supplied on application to Stations, Official Railway Agents, or to Mr. L. A. METCALF, District Commercial Manager, Leicester. Telephone 23841, Extn. 34; or to Mr. H. BULLOUGH, District Commercial Manager, Derby. Telephone: Derby 42442, Extn. 204; or Mr. A. S. MEAD, District Passenger Manager, 43 Smallbrook, Ringway, Birmingham. Telephone: MIDland 2711.

May, 1962
BR35000

(PX2/Adex)

LONDON MIDLAND

Arthur Gaunt & Sons (Printers) Ltd., Heanor, Derbyshire.

done properly the brakes would be dragging and some titanic struggles up the branch would ensue. On one occasion this happened to Ron Smith and myself and we were over time at Woodford while we pulled the strings ourselves to get the brakes released. As we were about to leave Rugby, Ron decided to 'have a go', as he was a driver who hated to be late in Leicester. Our engine was Standard '5' 4-6-0 No 73066 — a beautiful performer and possibly the best of the five at Leicester. We thrashed our way out of Rugby station and were up to 60mph by the time we reached the girder bridge over the LNWR main line. The noise as we hammered up Shawell bank was music indeed and we kept it going through the Lutterworth dip and up the final rise to Ashby Magna. On we flew down the bank and, although the line speed limit was 75mph, our speedometer was registering over 90mph approaching Whetstone! We finally screeched to a halt in Leicester with a 'GC Stop', and a railway enthusiast rushed up to the engine to congratulate us on running the 20 miles from Rugby in a little over 17min!

The Sunday only train was another good out-and-home mileage turn for Leicester. Originally we used to relieve Darnall men and take the Darnall 'B1' to Swindon and back, when we would be relieved, and so the engine did the round trip in a day. Later the diagram was altered, and we took a Leicester engine to Swindon. We would be relieved by Swindon men who took our engine on shed, while we had our meal break. If the engine ever failed at Swindon, as odd ones did, the Western Region would try to get rid of a Standard '5' which they disliked, but if this wasn't possible and the replacement engine was a 'Hall' 4-6-0, a Swindon driver would be sent with us as far as Oxford to make sure that we could handle the engine! In fact, summer Saturdays brought many different diagrams for Leicester shed, with workings to many places not normally visited. One such train was for Cleethorpes, with a conductor driver from Kirkby South Junction. The train travelled via Mansfield and Lincoln. Another working was the Llandudno which, after learning the road, Leicester men worked to Uttoxeter by the way of Derby Friargate and Eggington Junction. I must mention the working on this train as it was a real 'Round the World' turn for us. After relief at Uttoxeter, our next job would be to relieve a Kings Norton-Skegness train at Burton-on-Trent. As there was no direct route now from Uttoxeter to Burton, we had to go via Derby Midland. We relieved Saltley men on the Skegness train, which we would then work to Nottingham Victoria. After arrival we would uncouple and take the engine to Colwick shed. We then travelled back to Nottingham and finally completed our day by travelling 'on the cushions' on the 'South Yorkshireman' back to Leicester. I wonder if any other depot had a diagram where they visited both Derby stations in one day? Incidentally, we completed all this without making any overtime!

On Saturdays also there were about five weeks when Wembley Stadium staged various matches, such as Women's Hockey, the Rugby League Final, Schoolboys' Football and the FA Cup Final. These days always brought lots of work for Leicester, and very often this would mean lodging away. This meant one would work up with an early train, book off at Neasden, and lodge, before booking on again at night to work a late train back. When the line was still under Eastern Region control, we would be booked to lodge at Neasden, where strangely there was no lodging house. The men would

usually get their heads down in the coaches in Neasden sidings after a visit to The Pantiles pub. After the London Midland Region took over the GC, we would usually be booked to lodge at Kentish Town, where we would have to sign in at the lodge house to qualify for our lodging allowance. The best one could hope for was to be booked with Driver Arthur Dodd. Arthur's mother lived at Dudding Hill, close to Neasden, and after booking off at Neasden shed, Arthur would take his mate to his mother's house. Here you could enjoy a hot bath, a few hours sleep in a good bed, and usually a delightful tea, often topped off with raspberries and cream!

As regards 'foreign' engines and stock, we very rarely came across these on the GC, apart from the Southern Region stock on the Bournemouth-York trains. To locomotive men, any engine not from their own depot was a 'foreigner', even those from GC depots such as Woodford or Annesley. In this context, we did handle a few foreign engines. Perhaps the best examples were the Newcastle 'V2s' which arrived at Leicester on a certain car sleeper train. Leicester would always 'pinch' a trip out of them before they returned home the following night. They would usually be very well maintained engines, and I remember one in particular, No 60808 with 'Radar Ron' on the York-Bournemouth. We left Leicester 8min late and arrived in Banbury 7min before time! It was definitely the fastest I ever shot through Catesby tunnel in the up direction.

Many other special trains ran — very often they were factory outings to various places such as Bourne End, Marlow or Windsor, where the party would usually enjoy a boat trip on the River Thames and return from London late at night. (In fact in one instance we actually returned from Paddington, due to Marylebone being swamped with 'Starlight Specials'). I remember well one such trip to Windsor with one of Leicester's characters, George Evinson. Our steed was BR Standard '4' 4-6-0 No 75057, and we picked up our party from a local hosiery firm, at Lutterworth. Our outward route was via Banbury, Oxford and Didcot, where we joined the GW main line southward to Slough and there the branch to Windsor.

A very amusing incident occurred during this trip. The GW pilotman we picked up at Oxford declined George's offer of the controls and, instead, stood behind him to explain the road. As we came round the junction at Didcot we were routed on to the relief line, just as the London bound 'Red Dragon' went up the main line headed by a 'Britannia' Pacific. As we had a clear road, we were soon up to our line speed, striding along in fine style. To my amazement, the rear end of the express, far from disappearing in the distance, was actually getting closer! This spurred George on to open out the engine, and we were soon overhauling the other train. We were just beginning to pass the tender end of the 'Britannia', when we were slowed by adverse signals at Reading, and never had another chance to catch them. I would loved to have seen the reaction of the 'Britannia's' crew, had our little Standard '4' actually passed them! After arrival at Windsor, we returned to Slough shed to service our engine and work the train back in the evening. Our return was via the now long-defunct single line from Maidenhead via Bourne End which joined the joint line at High Wycombe. Although we were on duty for 15 hours, it was a very enjoyable day indeed. These trips were somewhat spoiled after the Midland Region took over. For instance, I later worked to Bourne End with a similar train and, after being relieved by GW men, we returned home as passengers. Before we were halfway home, a second set of men had already left Leicester 'on the cushions' to fetch the special back. On two other occasions on Windsor trains, we were relieved at High Wycombe, and travelled home on the 12.15 from Marylebone.

Another special train that used to run in the 1950s was the 'City of Leicester Holiday Express'. This train used to run to a different holiday resort on each day from Monday to Friday, and passengers could get a cheap rate by booking for all the five days. The itinerary would usually include London, Skegness, Scarborough and one or two of the south coast resorts. On 11 August 1958, Driver Alf Scott and myself really 'clicked' by being booked to work this train through to Brighton. We left Leicester with 'Black Five' No 44821 and a huge round headboard proclaiming to all what train we were. Our route was via the 'new line' through High Wycombe and, after picking up our SR pilot driver at Kensington Olympia, we headed for Clapham Junction and the electrified line to the south coast resort. We had taken water on West Ruislip troughs and so had a sufficient quantity for the journey. We were relieved on arrival at Brighton by men from the local depot who took our engine on shed to be serviced while Alf and I enjoyed the delights of the sea front for a couple of hours before rejoining our steed in the station. Our day was completed in 13 hours, but the number of miles worked on the mileage system meant that we received over 25 hours' pay! A good day indeed.

Another source of traffic that we worked in the season were the pigeon specials which used to run to various points for the birds to be released. These would usually be quite heavily loaded trains, consisting of up to 14 bogie vans. Whilst working such a train back from Sheffield one night, again with Ron Smith and 'V2' No 60863, we were forging up Staveley Bank when, to our consternation, we found the automatic signals between Staveley and Duckmanton were against us. It was a night of persistent drizzling rain, and we didn't give much for our chances of starting the 450-ton train again. I telephoned the signalman, who informed me that he

was 'bagging' a laggardly freight at Duckmanton to allow us to pass. I told him that I would ring back if we required a banker from Staveley. When we eventually got the road, we strode away in fine style, apart from one initial slip, with the sanders working to good effect. On passing the freight Ron whistled the time honoured 'long and a short', which all railwaymen will understand, while I gave the thumbs up sign to the Duckmanton signalman. Whenever I hear recordings of the 'V2s' slogging up the Waverley route, it always brings back memories of nights such as this.

On another special train, an incident occurred that seems unbelievable even now. Driver Horace Clifford and myself were working back from Nottingham Victoria to Leicester with a train from Skegness, with which we were booked to stop at most of the intermediate stations. Before leaving Nottingham the guard would ensure that any passengers for the intermediate stations were seated in the front five coaches. We would then stop at each station with the front five alongside the platform, thereby alleviating the need to draw forward.

On the night in question we had left Ruddington and were heading up the bank towards our next port of call at Rushcliffe Halt. We were just short of Gotham Sidings when we suddenly lost the vacuum, the brake coming full on. We could not figure out what had caused it and when we recreated the vacuum and started to move again the brake was immediately reapplied. 'It must be the guard', said Horace, so I set off to the rear end to find out what was wrong. On arriving at the rear of our train, I could not believe what I saw. Our guard, who was one of the many Indians then appearing on BR, was actually handing down from the train a man, woman and two children who had missed their station, so that they could walk back in the dark to Ruddington! As a man who had been brought up to the sound railway tradition that the safety of the passenger took priority over everything else, I was staggered. I told the family to get back in the train and carry on to Rushcliffe, where the railway would have to make arrangements to get them home. When we stopped there I explained to the porter what had happened, and a taxi was indeed provided to ferry the family home.

Left:
'Jubilee' No 45562 *Alberta* approaches the remains of Duckmanton South Junction near Staveley on the GC main line with the 09.55 (SO) Leeds City-Poole express on 1 August 1964. *J. S. Hancock*

'Starlight Specials' and sleepers

One good source of revenue for the railways in the 1950s was the series of overnight workings known as 'Starlight Specials' which ran from various London termini to Scotland. Passengers had to book throughout from London to Scotland at a very attractive rate. The GC line worked a number of these trains, with Leicester crews being well involved in their running.

After working up to Marylebone with the 14.10 from Manchester on Saturdays only instead of travelling home passenger, we would in the summer timetable work back with a 'Starlight' through to Nottingham Victoria, where we would be relieved, and return home as passengers. On one occasion, when I was rostered with Driver Lou Bennett, Neasden shed was short of engines so we agreed to return with our own, which on this occasion was 'V2' No 60879. We simply filled up the firebox and topped up the tender with coal, before storming back to Nottingham. Incidentally, having rushed back with this train on the Saturday night, Lou went for his regular eyesight test at Derby on the following Monday and failed owing to colour blindness!

Leicester men also worked the 'Starlights' northwards from Leicester, usually being relieved at Darnall, where the trains went round the Attercliffe curve, for York. However, on one particular train we went through to York with a Darnall pilot driver. The usual power was a York 'V2' but it was not unusual to get a 'B16' 4-6-0 when the motive power department was short of engines.

Other summer service trains were the car-sleepers. The one that Leicester were mostly involved with was the 19.10 Marylebone-Stirling train. After working up with the 14.14 all stations from Leicester, we would after relief at Harrow-on-the-Hill, travel to Neasden shed to pick up our engine for the return working. After the closure of Neasden, we had to learn the road to Cricklewood, where the engines were then being serviced. In the latter days, the engine would almost invariably be a Holbeck 'Jubilee' 4-6-0 and usually a very well maintained one at that.

Before the days of the Neasden closure, Ron Smith and I made quite a *faux pas* in June 1960 while working the 'Stirling' with 'Black Five' No 45059. The signalling at Ashendon Junction where the GC route diverged from the GW line had then recently been altered from semaphore to colour light operation, and Ron had obviously not read his special instructions carefully enough. When diverging to the GC route, the distant signal would show a yellow indication and the junction signal would remain at red until the train reached the track circuit that controlled it, whereupon it would change to green, with a row of white lights indicating the route. This was to make sure that the train speed was brought down to 45mph for the junction. On the night in question, we were rushing down from Haddenham, and noticed that all the signals at Ashendon were showing green. Ron said to me, 'He's seen us taking the junction at the right speed all week, mate, so he's giving us a run through tonight'. We had just started braking for the junction, when Ron realised that the route indicator lights were not showing. 'We're going to Banbury' he shouted, slamming the brakes full on. Alas, we overshot the junction, finally stopping a full train length round the flyover of the GW route. I immediately ran back towards the box, where I saw the signalman frantically waving to us to set back our train. When I got within earshot he said, 'Sorry, mate, I thought you were the 7.10 from Paddington'. By the time we had set back over the points, and got our train heading in the right direction, the little episode had cost us 10min delay. Although we recovered all the time to Leicester, our Guard insisted on reporting the incident, so unfortunately we had to appear before the Shed Master, who pointed out in no uncertain terms where we had gone wrong. An amusing turn to the proceedings came after we had been relieved at Leicester. As we were walking down the platform, we heard a man on the train telling a porter that 'We went the wrong way, down a little single line'.

'Someone else who knows the Western', I thought.

As stated previously, after the closure of Neasden shed, GC line engines were stabled and serviced at Cricklewood. The usual power at this time on the car sleeper was a Holbeck engine which would work through from Leeds to Marylebone and return with the following night's train. These engines, normally a 'Jubilee', but occasionally the unnamed

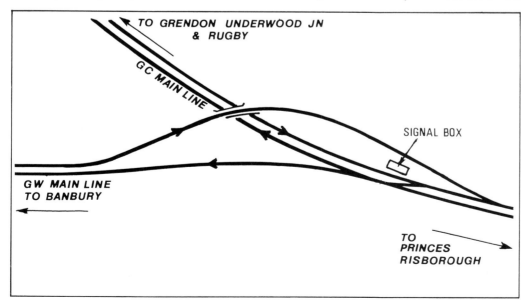

Left:
Ashendon Junction track plan.

TO GRENDON UNDERWOOD JN & RUGBY

GC MAIN LINE

SIGNAL BOX

GW MAIN LINE TO BANBURY

TO PRINCES RISBOROUGH

Left:
'B1' 4-6-0 No 61225 'dive bombs' through Ashendon Junction and passes under the up GW Birmingham-Paddington line with a Hastings-Sheffield Express on 27 August 1955. This Leicester engine would have taken over the train at Kensington Olympia.
C. Creer

Above:
A shot of the final Bournemouth-York express to run over the GC passing Bulwell Common's North Junction, headed by Brush Type 4 (now Class 47) diesel D1572 on the last day of through operation — 3 September 1966. *J. Cupit*

Left:
A Saturdays-only Skegness-Leicester train is worked out of Nottingham Victoria by rebuilt 'Jubilee' No 45735 *Comet* on 29 August 1964. The train is the 15.41 (SO) Skegness-Leicester. '9F' 2-10-0 No 92069 awaits to take over the following 16.39 Mablethorpe-Leicester. *J. S. Hancock*

Left:
**'Jubilee' No 45694
Bellerophon is about to
depart from Nottingham
Victoria with the 10.34
(SO) Bournemouth-
Bradford on 9 July 1963.
The clock tower in the
background is all that now
remains of the station.**
J. S. Hancock

'Britannia' No 70047, were usually in very good condition, and I enjoyed some great trips on this train. We also worked this train northwards from Leicester as far as Rotherham Masborough. To allow the train to reach Midland metals, our route was via the 'clog and knocker' or more correctly, the LDEC route. This left the GC main line at Kirkby South Junction just north of Annesley tunnel, and went via Shirebrook and 'over the mountains' to Clowne. At Killamarsh, we joined the Midland line from Tapton Junction to Rotherham.

The normal load on this train was 14 coaches, and the 'Jubilee' would be heard to marvellous effect on the steep gradients of this route. I remember one night in July 1963, with Driver Sid 'Kamakaze' Cooper, we were blasting our way up to the summit at Clowne box with 'Jubilee' No 45608 *Gibraltar*, when the engine suddenly lost her footing and started to slip violently. The signalman who had been watching our progress from his open box window suddenly shot back inside his cabin and slammed shut the window, as the 'Jaffas' rained down on him like meteorites. It was a good job we had finished most of the hard work, as half the contents of the firebox had disappeared up the chimney. On our return with the up train with No 45562 *Alberta* as our steed, we were stopped at Killamarsh and told to proceed with caution to Clowne, as some platelayers had had to be called out to fight a raging bank fire. 'What mad devil started that then?' asked Sid innocently!

As previously stated, the 'Jubilees' were well tested on this train, and it was unusual to find a poor one out of the large number at Holbeck at this particular time. This is praise indeed, coming from a GC man.

Although not strictly a special train, another sleeping car express worked by Leicester men was a London-Manchester train diverted from the LNWR main line during its electrification. For this working, which was diagrammed for Class 7 power, 'Royal Scot' 4-6-0s were sent to Annesley shed. They went to Annesley because Nottingham Victoria was chosen as the location where the Newton Heath Type 4 diesel which had hauled the train from Manchester would be replaced by a steam locomotive. Some of the original stud, such as Nos 46126 and 46143 were very poor examples indeed, being already worn out when they were received. For instance, No 46143 needed two full tanks of water to travel from London to Leicester.

Later on some much better machines arrived — Nos 46122/56/58/67 being particularly good examples. Unfortunately, these gradually became run down themselves, with maintenance perhaps not being quite as good as it could be. Nevertheless, I enjoyed some good times on the 'Royal Scots' working the 12.30 from Marylebone. Although they suffered the usual injector problems at times, they were not so bad as the 'Black Fives' in this respect. I have been in Leicester as much as 12min before time with drivers such as Len Woodhead and Maurice Hutchinson. This proves that if an engine is in 'good nick', no matter what its parentage, a driver will quite happily run his train, even though he obviously enjoys it more on an engine with which he is familiar.

The firing techniques required on the 'Royal Scots', were very different to those used on the 'V2s' and 'A3s'. Where we had been used to a short, wide firebox on the Gresley engines, we were now confronted with a long, narrow one, which needed firing correctly to maintain steam pressure. After the GC firemen got used to the 'Scots', they put up some very good performances on the sleeper.

Incidentally, I have often heard jibes about the 17.15 Nottingham Victoria-Marylebone needing a Class 7 engine to haul seven coaches, but this was in fact the up working which was used to send up the engine that worked from Marylebone to Nottingham with the 00.30 sleeper. Sometimes one could encounter unusual power on the sleeper, especially after Willesden shed assumed responsibility for the servicing of GC line engines in London. If Woodford men failed the engine on the up train, Willesden would appropriate anything they could lay their hands on. I have worked the train with Western Division 'Britannias' such as No 70017 *Arrow* and even on one occasion with 'Jubilee' No 45742 *Connaught* which still bore its Carlisle Kingmoor shedplate. At the other end of the line, Annesley would also pinch engines such as York 'V2s' if they could not find a 'Scot' fit enough to work the job.

This train was perhaps Leicester shed's 'last fling' on express work as by the end of 1963 most of the fast workings they had been employed on were extinct apart from the few trains that they encountered in the summer season, and a few runs between Rugby and Nottingham Victoria.

CROSS-COUNTRY SERVICES FROM LEICESTER CENTRAL

SUMMER SATURDAYS: 15 JUNE 1959 to 13 SEPTEMBER 1959

LEICESTER CENTRAL

Depart 23.55   Rugby Central, Woodford Halse, Banbury General, Basingstoke, Portsmouth & Southsea, Portsmouth Harbour arr 04.13 (from Sheffield Victoria dep 22.00)

Depart 00.05   Rugby Central, Woodford Halse, Banbury General, Basingstoke, Portsmouth & Southsea, Portsmouth Harbour arr 04.23 (from Nottingham Victoria dep 23.30). (18 July to 29 August)

Depart 01.00   Lutterworth, Rugby Central, Whitstable & Tankerton, Herne Bay, Birchington, Westgate, Margate, Broadstairs, Ramsgate arr 06.19 (18 July to 15 August)

Depart 01.30   Lutterworth, Rugby Central, Woodford Halse, Whitstable & Tankerton, Herne Bay, Birchington, Westgate, Margate, Broadstairs, Dumpton Park, Ramsgate arr 06.51 (from Derby Friargate dep 23.35). (Until 15 September)

Depart 01.50   Rugby Central, Woodford Halse, Brighton, Eastbourne, Bexhill, St Leonards West Marina, St Leonards Warrior Square, Hastings 07.35 (from Sheffield Victoria dep 23.40). (4 July to 29 August)

Depart 02.12   Rugby Central, Woodford Halse, Banbury General, Swindon arr 05.45 (from York dep 22.22)

Depart 03.24   Rugby Central, Banbury General, Oxford, Basingstoke, Southampton, Brockenhurst, New Milton, Bournemouth Central 08.16 (from Nottingham Victoria dep 02.45)

Depart 05.20   Loughborough Central, Nottingham Victoria, stations to Derby Friargate, to Llandudno arr 10.54 (4 July to 10 September)

Depart 07.45   Loughborough Central, Arkwright Street, Nottingham Victoria, New Basford, Bulwell Common, Hucknall Central, Mansfield Central to Scarborough Londesborough Road arr 13.25 (20 June, 29 August, 5 September only)

Depart 08.25   Loughborough Central, Arkwright Street, Nottingham Victoria to Scarborough Londesborough Road arr 13.25 (27 June to 22 August)

Depart 13.26   Woodford Halse, Oxford, Basingstoke, Winchester City, Southampton, Brockenhurst, New Milton, Christchurch, Pokesdown, Bournemouth Central, Poole arr 18.20 (from Bradford dep 10.15)

Depart 13.40   Rugby Central, Banbury General, Oxford, Reading West, Basingstoke, Winchester City, Eastleigh, Southampton Central, Brockenhurst, New Milton, Christchurch, Pokesdown, Boscombe, Bournemouth Central, Bournemouth West arr 18.53 (from Newcastle dep 08.35)

Depart 13.59   Rugby Central, Banbury General, Oxford, Basingstoke, Eastleigh, Southampton, Brockenhurst, New Milton, Christchurch, Pokesdown, Boscombe, Bournemouth Central arr 19.16 (from Sheffield Victoria dep 12.10)

Depart 15.28   Rugby Central, Banbury General, Oxford, Swindon, Newport, Cardiff General, Bridgend, Port Talbot, Neath, Swansea High Street arr 21.10 (from Newcastle dep 10.08)

Depart 22.38   Lutterworth, Rugby Central, Woodford Halse, Banbury General to Swindon arr 02.00 (from York dep 18.40 and Scarborough dep 17.30) (11 July to 12 September)

Left:
The BR '9F' 2-10-0s could 'run with anything' as was proved on both the GC and the Somerset & Dorset line. Here No 92154 climbs towards Belgrave & Birstall, and is just passing its down distant signal, with an excursion for Mablethorpe on 3 August 1964. *Ian Allan Library*

Top:
Driver Ted Rodwell, who was involved with Frank Stratford in a collision at Lutterworth, heads through Ashby Magna with smartly turned-out 'Black Five' No 45062 on a Loughborough-Wembley Hill FA Cup Final Special on 25 May 1963.
M. Mitchell

Above left:
Wembley-bound supporters again. Nottingham Forest fans are pictured emerging from Ashby Magna tunnel behind 'B1' 4-6-0 No 61041 (the first unnamed example) on 2 May 1959.
B. O. Hilton

Left:
Frank Stratford looks back at the camera as, with the 'Kamakaze' at the regulator, 'Black Five' 4-6-0 No 45342 heads a Wembley-bound load of Leicester City supporters into the short 'Ashby Tunnel' on 25 May 1963. The train is the 09.35 Leicester-Wembley and the unusually late date for the FA Cup Final was due to the severe winter causing the football season to be extended for two weeks.
B. O. Hilton

Right:
The 'Western Connection'. 'L1' 2-6-4T No 67789 waits to leave Banbury with the 13.50 to Woodford Halse on 25 August 1960. The 'modern' station is largely intact today — a modern monument to the many GC services that once passed through. *M. Mensing*

Below:
'Royal Scot' 4-6-0 No 46167 *The Hertfordshire Regiment* makes a fine sight running through the deep cutting away from Rugby Central with an up special on 26 October 1963. *P. Riley*

Right:
Brush Type 4 (now Class 47) diesel D1865 passes the site of the demolished Braunston & Willoughby station with a Newcastle-Poole train on 7 July 1966. *M. Mitchell*

86

Top:
GWR 'Grange' 4-6-0 No 6864 *Dymock Grange* calls at Leicester Central on 6 August 1955 with a train from Bournemouth and Poole. No 6864 is about to uncouple from the train, be turned and return south on another working. The train would then be taken on by a Leicester engine. *J. F. Henton*

Above:
Engine changing at Banbury. 'V2' No 60893 has just taken over from 'Hall' 4-6-0 No 6930 *Aldersey Hall* (right) to work forward with the 10.25 Poole-Bradford on 6 August 1960. *M. Mensing*

Above:
The long-standing Sheffield-Swindon (Sundays only) service, which was worked by a Leicester crew to Swindon, is seen headed by 'B1' 4-6-0 No 61271 having just breasted the summit between Eydon Road and Chacombe Road on the Banbury branch on 1 March 1959. *M. Mitchell*

Left:
On 9 May 1964, Stanier 'Coronation' No 46251 *City of Nottingham* ran down the GC line on a rail tour. Here she storms out of Catesby tunnel near Charwelton with the RCTS 'East Midlander' comprised of immaculate ex-LMS coaches. Driver George Neat is at the regulator. *M. Pope*

Below:
Leicester 'V2' No 60890 drifts round the High Wycombe curves with a Women's Hockey Special for Wembley Hill on 11 March 1961. Note the banner repeaters for the signals needed because of the curvature at High Wycombe. *H. Harman*

Above:
Western connection. Aylesbury in August 1960 sees GWR 0-6-0PT No 6429 taking water while in charge of the Princes Risborough auto-train. Many branch services ran through to High Wycombe and even Maidenhead via the now-closed High Wycombe-Bourne End line. Note the stern warning about smoke nuisance on the water column. *G. C. Farnell*

Below:
The local push-pull service from Aylesbury is seen at Princes Risborough with 0-6-0PT No 5420 in charge in August 1960. *G. C. Farnell*

Top:
'B1' 4-6-0 No 61201 climbs between High Wycombe and Saunderton with an empty stock working to Leicester from Marylebone in June 1957. *G. C. Farnell*

Above left:
An up excursion for London with 'B1' No 61408 in charge, rushes through Princes Risborough in May 1959. *G. C. Farnell*

Left:
GWR '61xx' 2-6-2T No 6142 waits to depart for Princes Risborough and High Wycombe from Aylesbury Town in July 1960. Some trains ran straight to Paddington, and as the Prairie is wearing 'Express' lamps, she must indeed be bound for the Western Region's London terminus.
G. C. Farnell

Marylebone Memories

Frank Stratford

I myself was a victim of the run down of the Great Central line, being made redundant in December 1963. By February 1964 I had transferred to the wrongly named Marylebone diesel depot. I say wrongly named, as the depot still worked a high proportion of steam turns at this time. I think the title came about with the closure of Neasden shed, and the dieselising of the suburban services, projecting a modern image. In fact, Les Newman, who transferred to the depot after 25 years on electrics at Watford Junction, was staggered to find he would be back on steam, which he had almost forgotten after so long! He said it gave him a new lease of life!

My move to Marylebone quickly brought home to me the difference in the seniority positions at different depots. Whereas I had been redundant at Leicester after 12 years of service, I now found that Marylebone depot had men with only five years' service who were already passed firemen. As promotion on BR was strictly on a seniority basis, it now meant that my name had to be put forward to pass the inspector. I duly went with Inspector Fred Ansell from the Midland's Cambridge Street depot on Wednesday and Thursday, 19-20 February 1964. A full day was spent answering questions on rules and regulations, signals and all the various working parts of the steam locomotive, and the second day was spent on actually driving trains out on the road. For the passenger train run, Fred used to take his candidate out to Aylesbury and then observe him 'at the Johnson bar' up to Marylebone on the 08.15 from Nottingham Victoria. When the train rolled in, I was met by two well-known characters — 'Royal Scot' No 46163 *Civil Service Rifleman* on the footplate of which was Woodford

Driver 'Fritz' Fennell. Everything went swimmingly, with yours truly at the controls, and I well remember that, as we actually stopped in Marylebone, the huge digital clock clattered over to show 11.25 — our correct arrival time. I really felt pleased, as 'Fritz' said to the inspector 'You've got to hand it to these Leicester men — neither 11.24½ nor 11.25¼, but 11.25 dead on — that's driving!'

After another session with Fred in the 'classroom', he informed me that I could go home and tell the wife that I could now move to the other side of the cab. Shortly after this, I had to attend the diesel school at Derby and then have road training on the DMUs, so that I could be utilised on the suburban services.

So started a very happy two years in my railway career. The suburban services to Aylesbury and Princes Risborough were very well run with the DMUs, although rather hectic at times. It was a bit unusual at first, being on my own working a train, but I soon got used to it and, in fact, came to enjoy working the DMUs. The Aylesbury service was very sharp and to run to time the units had to be driven at their hardest, and the braking left until the last moment. For instance, when galloping down to Great Missenden or Wendover, power would still be on until after passing the distant signal with the set careering along at its 70mph maximum. A full application of the brakes for a short period soon brought the speed down, and it was only occasionally that I misjudged and ran past by half a coach. The brake fitters at Marylebone were very good and would be constantly taking up and reblocking the brakes, and one could have great confidence in the unit's ability to stop when required.

The trains to High Wycombe and Princes Risborough never seemed to be quite as hectic as on the Aylesbury 'Jazz', although in the morning and evening rush hour periods you

Top:
A scene still possible today sees 'B1' 4-6-0 No 61051 at Loughborough Central with the 16.38 Marylebone-Nottingham Victoria on 15 August 1964. *D. Holmes*

Right:
The DMU which took over the 08.15 Marylebone-Nottingham Victoria working is seen on its return journey with the 12.30 from Nottingham between Whetstone and Ashby Magna on 8 February 1964. The M1 motorway now dominates the scene to the right of the train. *M. Mitchell*

only needed one unit to be a bit laggardly and things would soon start to get a bit chaotic with trains blocking back, and the commuters getting a little agitated. All things considered, the DMUs did a good job and at the time of writing were still working over 20 years later.

Marylebone depot still worked plenty of local freight trains which were all steam-hauled until later on, when we trained on the Type 2 Bo-Bo diesels known as 'Fruit Machines' (later to become the Class 24s). The steam locomotives employed were the BR Standard '4' 2-6-0s numbered in the 76000 series, which I consider were possibly one of the best of the Standard classes I have worked on. They would steam freely however one fired them, and were really strong pullers. We used to work the morning trip from Aylesbury to Quainton Road, where we shunted the yards, and returned with the pick-up. We also worked coal to the Metropolitan yard at Willesden Green station, and the slack to Neasden Metropolitan sidings for their power station. This job entailed working out to Harrow-on-the-Hill, where we ran round our train in the yard and then worked back over the Metropolitan electric tracks to Neasden yard, laughable really, as one could have walked across from Neasden GC to the Metropolitan in 5min, but Harrow was the nearest point at which it was possible to gain access to the 'juice' tracks.

Another freight turn that I used to enjoy working was the afternoon trip from Aylesbury that originally went to Woodford yard until its closure, after which it was then routed via the Oxford-Bletchley line at Calvert to Swanbourne sidings, near Bletchley. Our return working on this trip was the aforementioned power station slack, and we would regularly be loaded to a 'full digger' which really made the Standard '4' Moguls cough a bit. I once had to use full cut-off and a wide-open regulator to get this train on the move again, after being held by signals on the flyover at Northolt Junction. The sound was unbelievable, and Marylebone Driver Horace 'Doctor' Bode, who lived close to Northolt Park station, swore blind that the vibration rocked him out of bed!

As stated previously though, I never saw one of these engines beaten and they were more than capable of working any of the trains at Marylebone. The pack that worked the Marylebone line were, I believe, Nos 76035-76044, and all of them seemed to be equally as good as one another.

Another freight train worked by Marylebone men, was the pick-up which ran down the Metropolitan branch to Chesham and also shunted the yard at Watford Metropolitan. I had to learn the routes to all these places on the Metropolitan, as all of them were new to me. Later on, when we had received diesel training, the Class 24 diesels used to be employed on these trains and had to be specially fitted with trip cocks for working over the electrified lines, as did the Standard '4s'. These were a safeguard to stop the train if a driver passed a signal at red. Until the guards got used to the loads allowed for these diesels, a few harrowing times were experienced by Marylebone men. One young passed fireman, Colin Parker, accepted his guard's word that they had 'just a full load' on and promptly lost control of the train after breasting the summit at Amersham. The train ran away down the bank through Chorleywood, Chalfont and Rickmansworth, control only being regained on the rising grade at Moor Park. He told me afterwards, his heart was in his mouth but, as luck would have it, he saw nothing but clear signals all the way. It is not a very nice feeling when you know you can not stop when required.

As far as passenger services were concerned, steam was still in evidence on various trains, including the 00.30

| YOUR REF. | | BRITISH RAILWAYS | | OUR REF. | PF | B.R. 3/2 |
| DATED | | L.M. REGION | | DATE | 26.2.64 | |

TO

Fireman F. H. Stratford
Marylebone

(Centre No.   )

FROM

Diesel Depot
Marylebone

Extn.   (Centre No.   )

FIREMAN FOR PASSING TO ACT AS DRIVER

Please note you are required to attend for medical examination at 10.10 am on Wednesday 4th March, 1964.

You should attend in uniform and I attach introductory note which you should hand to the Medical Officer, Second Floor, Euston House when keeping the appointment.

For a fireman to be passed for driving duties, it was necessary for him to undergo a medical examination in addition to other procedures. As can be seen from the original memorandum reproduced here, Author Frank Stratford was summoned to appear at Euston on 26 February 1964.

DEPOT SUPERINTENDENT

Manchester sleeper, the 03.40 from Marylebone, the 14.38 and 16.38 Marylebone-Nottingham departures and the 22.40 Manchester Mail. We were also utilised on some of the holiday trains if Cricklewood depot were short of drivers with route knowledge of the GC line. With the gradual decline of steam, I felt lucky to have been passed as a driver, for had I remained at Leicester, I would never have driven steam locomotives on the main line. My first time out on the main line as a driver was in fact on one of the summer service Eastbourne-Manchester holiday trains. I was booked to go to Cricklewood shed, pick up the engine and a fireman there, before proceeding light engine to Kensington Olympia to take over the train as far as Leicester.

On arrival at Cricklewood, I enquired of the Foreman as to what engine I had, and discovered it was something I had been weaned on — our old friend the 'B1'. It was No 61093 from Canklow — and a very decrepit looking steed it was too. The train was only booked to stop at Rugby but, seeing that the bottom plate of the water scoop was buckled up, I informed control that I would be stopping out of course at Princes Risborough for water. My mate then arrived, a young gentleman by the name of Nightingale who, when I enquired if he had ever fired one of these replied 'I've never seen one, what is it?' It was with some misgivings that I finally left the shed for Kensington. My first impressions of the locomotive were not wrong — it was a really rough one which rattled and banged in every joint. Mr Nightingale was not doing much singing, being in a hopeless state, trying to break the huge lumps of coal that were blocking the shovelling plate, and then trying to get the broken bits through the trap into the firebox. The exhaust steam injector on his side was not maintaining the boiler level very well either, so I finished up nursing the engine along, driving and firing it myself, shutting off down all the dips, and working the live steam injector on my side of the cab. I duly stopped for water as planned and we carried on to our Rugby stop. As we had lost some time, I now only had 20min for a 'right time' arrival in Leicester, so I decided to fill the firebox and do a 'Radar Ron' to Leicester, hoping that I could clear the bank at Shawell before we ran out of steam. I thrashed out of Rugby station and over the 'birdcage' bridge, hammering the 'B1' for all its worth. Imagine my surprise when I heard the safety valves start to lift. The engine was actually steaming better by being thrashed. We stormed up Shawell with the injector on and a full head of steam with the cut-off at 45%! On we roared through the Lutterworth dip until, on reaching Ashby Magna, I could afford to shut off steam as we were well up to time.

I managed to get my 'right time' arrival in Leicester and, after being relieved and showing my mate the way to Leicester Midland station for him to catch a train back to London, I went to see my wife and children who were still living in the Leicester area while I was in digs at the Hampden Club Railway Hostel in St Pancras. Incidentally, Fireman Nightingale, who was also at the same digs, packed up the job the following Monday and returned to his North Country home. He was obviously not a 'B1' fan!

I remember thinking at the time I was passed for driving that as the steam engine was obviously on its way out, I would be more than pleased if I could have one main line turn driving on steam. I did in fact go on to have 123 steam driving turns, including one Saturday night on the 22.40 Mail, when on our return from Leicester on the up train, which was diverted due to engineering work over the Aylesbury route, Fireman A. Botham and I ran from passing Aylesbury to stopping in Marylebone in 38min on 'Black Five' No 44685

Left:
BR '9F' 2-10-0 No 92160 pauses at Brackley Central with the 14.38 service for Nottingham Victoria on 3 August 1965. The 'Black Five' normally provided had failed and the '9F' was provided at short notice. *P. H. Wells*

Below:
Normal power for the 14.38 was a 'Black Five' at this time and here No 44941 prepares to leave Brackley Central for Nottingham on 13 April 1966. *P. H. Wells*

which was fitted with Skefko roller bearings. Even though some of the steam turns were on station pilot work and local freight, the bulk of my driving was spent on the main line, with many happy hours spent on the 03.40 from Marylebone, which we originally worked to Woodford but later took through to Leicester, returning with the 08.15 from Nottingham Victoria.

I was often booked on this turn with my old ex-Leicester mate, Keith West, who had recently arrived at Marylebone after a short spell at Cricklewood. Keith was a real enthusiast who, like myself, liked to run well. He would often fire me up by saying such things as 'Les Newman ran from Ashby to Leicester in 10min on this job'. 'Watch this then', I used to say and one can imagine the fun that ensued. I'm sure some of the passengers would hardly have settled over their newspapers before we were running into Leicester! It was not unusual to find any kind of engine on this turn as Willesden would send across anything they could lay hand to. On 30 July 1965 we were even treated to Southern based Class 5 No 73119 *Elaine*, but her nameplates had already been removed. On another occasion when returning from Leicester with the 08.15 from Nottingham Victoria with No 44780 and Fireman D. Harris, we treated a tape recording enthusiast to some really rousing starts from the station stops. On arrival in London we listened to a replay of the tape and I don't think I've heard one yet to beat it.

On another occasion, when working back from Woodford to Marylebone on 3 September 1965 with the 17.15 from Nottingham, Fireman Fitzsimmons and I were on 'Black Five' No 44869. We had just roared past Neasden South Junction when my mate noticed a door swinging open on the first coach. I brought the train to a stand at the automatic signals at Willesden Green and together we managed to close the slightly battered door. I informed the signalman by telephone that I would proceed with caution to Marylebone to save 'stopping the job'. On arrival I informed Control who now had to order the line to be searched back to Harrow-on-the-Hill, our last stop. It was only after arrival at Aylesbury that a DMU from Marylebone was seen to have had two coaches denuded of all their door handles by the courtesy of our swinging door!

On Saturdays only Marylebone men also worked the 16.38 to Leicester and travelled home as passengers. This job was a one-way ticket home for me, and I could usually get a swop to work this train, especially if I was booked on an earlier turn. The man who swopped with me would get an early finish, and I would get my ride home.

Although I left Marylebone before the last rites for the through trains, I did see the demise of the line, with sections 20 miles long, due to signalbox closures, men on the night mail having to telephone for help from a farm house, when their diesel failed, and the 16.38 being worked through to Nottingham with the diesel which had been station pilot, due to steam engine failure. It was terrible to witness the run-down of the GC, although it was a happy time for me at Marylebone, simply because it gave me two years of driving, which I might have otherwise missed. What also made it more interesting was the number of enthusiasts who travelled on the trains, as apart from Waterloo, Marylebone was the only London terminus with main line steam in operation at the time. We were regularly talked into 'having a go' and on

leaving Harrow-on-the-Hill some real 'dive bombing' would ensue, to try for a record time to Aylesbury!

I cannot leave the chapter on Marylebone without a few words on some of the characters I encountered there. I always found the cockneys a very friendly set of blokes, and some of the tales told about them are legion. There is the famous tale of the cockney driver who was getting relieved at Woodford. On the first day, the Woodford man complained bitterly about the amount of dust on the footplate. So the next morning, the Marylebone driver asked his mate to sweep it and then swill it down with the slacking pipe. Once again, the Woodford driver moaned, this time about the amount of water on the footplate. As quick as a flash, the cockney quipped 'What the hell do you want to die of mate — silicosis or bloody pneumonia?'

All the top link drivers I worked with were good mates, including Arthur Ross (one of life's gentlemen), George Jones, 'Doc' Bode, Bill Andrewes, Les Newman, Jimmy Griffiths and Bert Parker. Another well known character was Fred Brady who was always ready with a quick retort. One day in particular, he was running into Marylebone with a four-car DMU which was to couple up to a similar set which was already standing in the platform. The instructions for this manoeuvre were that the driver should first stop short of the set in the station, and make sure that nobody was working on it, before he buffered up. Most drivers usually just ran in and buffered up without stopping. On the day in question, Fred carried out the instructions correctly, at which Inspector Fred Ansell appeared from the stationary set to congratulate Fred, saying 'I wish all our drivers carried out the proper procedure'. Laconically Fred replied 'Oh, I normally buffer straight up, but I saw you in there, didn't I!'

I also became good friends with a real cockney character named Bill Strong, who was a No 5 link driver. Bill loved life and many were the pints we drank and games of darts we played after finishing duty. Our local was the Boston Arms at the back of Marylebone station which, in more recent years, was featured in television newscasts when the Balcombe Street siege was in progress. Unfortunately, my friendship with Bill turned out to be short-lived as he was tragically involved in a fatal accident while shunting the pick-up in the yard at Wendover on 16 October 1965.

An amusing incident happened just after Marylebone men had converted on to the DMUs. One of the faults that sometimes occurred on a DMU was the rupture of a No 7 fuse, the result of which was that the driver lost all control of the engine concerned. In this case, the driver had the job of isolating the engine and centralising the final-drive gearbox, to make it in effect a 'swinger'. When this happened for the first time to Sid Caley (known to all his friends as 'Chocolate', which older readers will understand, as Caleys was once a well known brand of chocolate bar), he was eager to find out if he had carried out all the procedures correctly, and made enquiries of the Mechanical Foreman. 'Oh yes' said the Foreman, 'You've done everything perfectly, except for one small thing'. 'What's that then?' asked Sid. 'You've isolated the wrong bloody engine!' retorted the Foreman.

My enjoyable days at Marylebone came to an end in March 1966 when, owing to the difficulty in obtaining accommodation for my wife and now swiftly growing three children, I reluctantly accepted a move to Leicester Midland depot. We still worked a few GC line trains, walking over to the Central station and relieving crews on some of the semi-fasts, before taking the train on to Nottingham Victoria. Otherwise, my time at Leicester Midland was rather uninteresting, consisting largely of diesel work, apart from one or two diversions. One day I was rostered on the West Bridge shunt, which meant I had now worked out of all four Leicester stations. Also, on Tuesday, 29 March 1966, I worked up the Enderby Quarry branch with '8F' 2-8-0 No 48528. Incidentally, this was the only real stretch of Midland & LNWR Joint line and went to my home town. The following week I worked the Wigston wagon shops shunt with BR Standard '2' 2-6-0 No 78028. What was destined to be my final turn on a steam engine occurred on 1 June 1966 and perhaps prophetically it involved a run over GC metals. The chord

line from the Midland to the GC had now been laid in and on the day in question we traversed this line on '8F' 2-8-0 No 48625 to shunt the petrol tanks at Abbey Lane sidings which at this time were still open. It was a coincidence indeed that my final steam turn was on GC metals, and also that Abbey Lane was involved, as I had spent many hours there on the shunt as a young passed cleaner.

I lingered on at Leicester Midland for a few more years and although some of the jobs such as to Crewe or Oldbury were interesting, I never really felt at home. In fact, GC men were known to their Midland counterparts as the 'invaders'. In April 1969, I finally 'took the golden handshake', and left BR service.

All through services were withdrawn from the Great Central main line on the night of 3/4 September 1966.

LOCOMOTIVE ALLOCATIONS – NEASDEN MPD

Date: 1955-56
Region: Eastern   '34E' NEASDEN, AYLESBURY AND CHESHAM
Shed Code: 34E

1473	60044	*Melton*	61206	67761	67782	69341	76043
42222	60050	*Persimmon*	67416	67762	67783	69350	76044
42225	60108	*Gay Crusader*	67418	67767	67786	69354	
42230	61001	*Eland*	67420	67768	67787	76035	
42231	61009	*Hartebeeste*	67740	67771	67788	76036	
42232	61028	*Umseke*	67747	67772	67792	76037	
42248	61077		67748	67773	67794	76038	
42249	61083		67749	67774	67795	76039	
42250	61116		67752	67778	67798	76040	
42251	61136		67753	67780	69315	76041	
42252	61164		67760	67781	69318	76042	
42256	61187						

Date: Summer 1959
Region: London Midland
Shed Code: 14D

1473	41272	42232	42253	42291	42588	44830	61136	76037	76043	80139
D3304	42157	42248	42256	42437	42595	44847	61187	76038	76044	80140
D3305	42222	42249	42281	42450	42618	45260	61206	76039	80059	80141
D3306	42225	42250	42282	42453	42629	45416	64955	76040	80083	80142
D3507	42230	42251	42283	42256	44691	61077	76035	76041	80137	80143
41270	42231	42252	42284	42568	44819	61116	76036	76042	80138	80144

Left:
BR Standard '4' 2-6-0 No 76041 is seen on pick-up freight duty at Sudbury Hill on 9 April 1965. The 2-6-0s remained on GC line trains in the London area up until the withdrawal of through workings. *W. Piggott*

LONDON MARYLEBONE TO NOTTINGHAM VICTORIA

WEEKDAYS, 7 SEPTEMBER 1964 to 13 JUNE 1965

					SO	A		SX		B	C	D
Marylebone	01.40		03.40	08.38			14.38		16.38		21.55	
Harrow-on-the-Hill				08.58			14.57		16.57		22.54	
Aylesbury Town			05.01						17.38		23.04	
			05.20	09.31			15.38		18.05		23.32	
Brackley Central			05.48	09.53			16.05				23.46	00.12
Woodford Halse			06.02	10.04			16.18		18.18	21.38	23.48	00.17
			06.50	10.06			16.20		18.20	21.41		
Rugby Central	03.22		07.11	10.24		15.35	16.39		18.39	22.02	00.09	00.38
	03.33		07.20	10.27	12.30	15.38	16.41	17.20	18.41	22.09	00.14	00.42
Lutterworth			07.31	10.36	12.41		16.52	17.31	18.52			
Ashby Magna			07.40	10.42	12.50		17.01	17.40	19.01			
Leicester Central	03.50		07.54	10.52	13.04	15.59	17.15	17.54	19.15	22.37	00.36	01.04
		07.30	08.05	10.56	13.08	16.04	17.19	18.00	19.24	22.48	00.48	01.15
Loughborough Central		07.44	08.19	11.07	13.22	16.16	17.31	18.14	19.36	23.02	01.02	01.29
		07.45	08.21	11.08	13.23	16.19	17.33	18.15	19.38	23.04	01.05	01.31
East Leake		07.54	08.30	11.15	13.32		17.42	18.24	19.47			
Nottingham Victoria		08.07	08.43	11.27	13.45	16.36	17.56	18.37	20.00	23.22	01.23	02.03

A: From Bournemouth West dep 10.50 to York arr 19.25
B: From Swindon dep 19.15 to Sheffield Victoria arr 00.47
C: To Manchester Piccadilly arr 04.07
D: From Swindon dep 09.50 to York arr 05.02

NOTTINGHAM VICTORIA TO LONDON MARYLEBONE

WEEKDAYS, 7 SEPTEMBER 1964 to 13 JUNE 1965

	A	B				C		SX	D
Nottingham Victoria	01.30	02.12	07.40	08.15	12.30	12.45	17.15	18.15	22.19
East Leake			07.54	08.29	12.42		17.29	18.29	
Loughborough Central	01.49	02.41	08.02	08.37	12.48	13.02	17.37	18.37	22.38
	01.50	03.00	08.04	08.38	12.50	13.04	17.39	18.39	22.40
Leicester Central	02.03		08.17	08.49	13.01	13.15	17.50	18.52	22.53
	02.18		08.20	08.52	13.05	13.18	17.54	18.55	23.07
Ashby Magna			08.36	09.08	13.17		18.10	19.11	
Lutterworth			08.45	09.17	13.25		18.19	19.20	23.27
Rugby Central	02.43		08.55	09.26	13.33	13.41	18.28	19.30	23.36
	02.47			09.30	13.35	13.44	18.29		23.42
Woodford Halse	03.10	03.47		09.50	13.53		18.49		00.05
	03.12	03.49		09.52	13.54		18.51		00.07
Brackley Central				10.06	14.06		19.04		
Aylesbury Town		04.23		10.29	14.27		19.27		
Harrow-on-the-Hill				11.09			20.09		
Marylebone		05.25		11.25	15.18		20.25		

A: From York dep 22.22 to Swindon arr 05.45
B: From Manchester Central
C: From York dep 10.08 to Bournemouth West arr 18.38
D: From York dep 18.40 to Swindon arr 02.18

Left:
'Royal Scot' 4-6-0 No 46125 *3rd Carabinier* passes Grendon Underwood Junction on 11 May 1964 with the 17.15 Nottingham Victoria-Marylebone. The line from Ashendon Junction can be seen running in on the left at the rear of the train.
M. Mensing

14.38 LONDON (MARYLEBONE) TO NOTTINGHAM VICTORIA

	Locomotive: Load Tons (Tare): Date:	'Royal Scot' No 46156 167 31 December 1963		Stanier '5' No 44665 135 8 December 1964		Stanier '5' No 44920 135 25 February 1965	
Distance *Miles*		*Minutes/* *seconds*	*Speeds* *(mph)*	*Minutes/* *seconds*	*Speeds* *(mph)*	*Minutes/* *seconds*	*Speeds* *(mph)*
0	MARYLEBONE	0.00	—	0.00	—	0.00	—
2¼	Canfield Place	5.12	31	5.18	28	4.53	38
5¼	Neasden South	8.41	55	9.42	53	9.30	50
9½	HARROW-ON-THE-HILL	14.09	—	15.57	—	15.46	—
10½	North Harrow	2.34	45	2.43	42	—	—
11¼	Pinner	3.44	52	3.52	51	4.03	45
13	Northwood Hills	5.22	48	5.28	48	5.42	49
14	Northwood	6.36	55	6.46	52	6.55	50
15¼	Moor Park	7.58	61	8.22	51	8.27	56
17½	Rickmansworth	11.05	25/36	11.18	25	11.07	33
19½	Chorley Wood	15.08	34	15.18	43	14.35	43
21¾	Chalfont	18.48	40	18.26	41	17.49	38
23¾	Amersham	22.12	64	21.18	41	21.13 21.27	sigs
28¾	Great Missenden	28.03	70	27.16	58	28.49	59
33½	Wendover	32.44	68	31.56	63	33.53	68
35¾	Stoke Mandeville	34.55	67	34.11	64	36.03	66
38	AYLESBURY	28.27	—	37.34	—	39.12	—
44¼	Quainton Road	9.31	43	8.16	58	8.07	53
47	Grendon Underwood	12.41	55	11.15	57	11.11	54
49	Calvert	14.42	62	13.18	62	13.13	66
54½	Finmere	20.44	65	19.00	68	18.32	69
59¼	BRACKLEY	25.26	—	24.20	—	23.43	—
62½	Helmdon	5.34	59	5.15	62	5.02	60
66	Culworth	9.16	72	8.52	56	8.36	61
67½	Culworth Junction	—	—	10.02	69	9.33	71
69	WOODFORD HALSE	12.26	—	12.22	—	11.45	—
71½	Charwelton	—	—	5.20	40	4.07	62
75	Staverton Road	—	—	9.20	63	8.01	eased
78¼	Braunston	—	—	12.07	76	11.16	62
83¼	RUGBY CENTRAL	—	—	16.53	—	16.33	—
86¾	Shawell	—	—	5.01	54	5.04	53
90	LUTTERWORTH	—	—	9.04	—	9.08	—
94	ASHBY MAGNA	—	—	6.38	—	6.18	—
98¼	Whetstone	—	—	8.10	53	5.56	60
102¼	Leicester South Goods	—	—	—	62	10.09	56
103	LEICESTER CENTRAL	—	—	11.38	—	11.49	—

No 46156 crewed by Driver Upton and Fireman Musgrave.
No 44920 crewed by Driver Needle and Fireman Coyles to Woodford; Driver Cave and Fireman Gregg to Leicester.

Logs by J. E. Green

17.15 NOTTINGHAM VICTORIA TO LONDON MARYLEBONE

		'Royal Scot' No 46163		Stanier '5' No 45416		Stanier '5' No 45190	
Locomotive:							
Load Tons (Tare):		196		196		228	
Date:		31 December 1963		8 December 1964		25 February 1965	
Distance Miles		Minutes/ seconds	Speeds (mph)	Minutes/ seconds	Speeds (mph)	Minutes/ seconds	Speeds (mph)
0	LEICESTER CENTRAL			0.00		0.00	
¾	Leicester South Goods	–	–	2.41	44	2.23	47
4¾	Whetstone	–	–	8.10	49	7.09	52
9	ASHBY MAGNA	–	–	13.53	–	12.55	–
13	LUTTERWORTH			0.00 / 7.47	45	0.00 / 7.41	45
17¼	Shawell	–	–	0.00 / 5.36	62	0.00 / 5.24	55
20¾	RUGBY CENTRAL	–	–	9.52	–	10.03	–
25¾	Braunston	–	–	0.00 / 6.44	58	0.00 / 6.50	58
29	Staverton Road	–	–	10.34	48	10.30	46
33½	Charwelton	–	–	15.30	57	13.36	56
36	WOODFORD HALSE	–	–	18.52	–	18.41	–
37½	Culworth Junction	0.00 / 3.30	50	0.00 / 3.47	47	0.00 / 3.34	47
39	Culworth	4.28	58	4.57	56	5.00	44
41½	Helmdon	8.36	60	9.03	58	9.08	58
45¼	BRACKLEY	12.00	–	13.17	–	13.13	–
51	Finmere	0.00 / 5.56	65	0.00 / 6.37	62	0.00 / 6.28	65
56½	Calvert	11.50	57	12.21	56	12.06	58
58½	Grendon Underwood	13.06	55	14.26	59	14.14	55
61¾	Quainton Road	16.21	57	17.38	56	17.34	62
68	AYLESBURY	23.36	–	25.27	–	24.26	–
71¼	Stoke Mandeville	0.00 / 4.35	41	0.00 / 4.58	35	0.00 / 4.48	40
73½	Wendover	7.45	49	9.05	33	9.45	43
77¼	Great Missenden	12.52	67	15.46	61	16.03	62
82¼	Amersham	18.12	58	22.06	44	22.09	41
84¼	Chalfont	20.15	62	24.49	50	24.43	55
86½	Chorley Wood	22.14	65	27.06	62	26.53	63
88½	Rickmansworth	25.34	25	29.48	25	29.37	37
89¾	Moor Park	28.37	56	33.09	41	33.38	36
91	Northwood	29.19	58	35.16	43	36.45	44
92	Northwood Hills	30.20	60	36.38	45	37.03	48
93¾	Pinner	32.29	64	38.19	46	38.43	48
94½	North Harrow	33.24	60	40.04	40	40.14	38
95½	HARROW-ON-THE-HILL	35.46	–	42.07	–	42.41	–
	Brent North	0.00 / 4.03	65	0.00 / 4.15	51	0.00 / 4.30	54
98¾	Neasden South	5.17	57	5.05	43	5.26	54
100¾	Canfield Place	9.24	slack	9.17	sigs stop	9.31	sigs stop
103	MARYLEBONE	15.47	–	16.34	–	16.32	–

No 45190 crewed by Driver Cave and Fireman Gregg of Woodford.

Logs by J. E. Green

Left:
Observed from the front of a Marylebone bound DMU, BR Standard '4' 2-6-0 No 76040 is seen taking oil tanks away from Marylebone diesel depot. Metropolitan and Bakerloo (now Jubilee) line trains are clearly seen on their own lines to the left.
G. C. Farnell

Below:
'B1' 4-6-0 No 61313 heads the 08.15 semi-fast from Nottingham Victoria through Quainton Road on August Bank Holiday Monday, 1960. These semi-fast services, which replaced the expresses, originally loaded to six coaches but as time went on they were reduced to four and even three.
G. C. Farnell

Facing page, top:
'B1' No 61206 stands on Aylesbury shed with a BR Standard '4' 2-6-0. Her 34E shedplate shows that she belongs to Neasden and Aylesbury sheds; she had worked a pick-up freight and was waiting to run back south to Neasden.
G. C. Farnell

Facing page, bottom:
Fairburn '4MT' 2-6-4T No 42230 attracts attention at Marylebone as water cascades from its overfilled tank. She had worked the train in from Aylesbury and the replacement locomotive had just backed on to the other end. The Fairburn tanks were supplemented by some of the BR Standard '4' variety, before the DMUs arrived. The date is September 1959. *G. C. Farnell*

Top left:
GWR '61xx' 2-6-2T No 6143 heads the Maidenhead, High Wycombe, Princes Risborough and Aylesbury stopper at Little Kimble. This service provided a useful link between the GW and GC lines, which is now impossible owing to the closure of the section between Bourne End and High Wycombe.
G. C. Farnell

Centre left:
'B1' 4-6-0 No 61106 arrives at Amersham with an 'ord' from Nottingham in March 1959. These long distance stoppers were common on the GC line. *G. C. Farnell*

Left:
'B1' 61106 is seen again on the same service — this time at Harrow-on-the-Hill, later in April 1959. The grime is still evident on the same spots on the boiler which suggests that no cleaning has occurred for at least a month!
G. C. Farnell

Above:

Standard '4' 2-6-4T No 80144 approaches Princes Risborough running bunker first on a suburban service from Marylebone in June 1957. The fireman looks out for the junction signals for the station. *G. C. Farnell*

Right:

BR Standard '4' 2-6-0 No 76039 had worked up to Woodford from Neasden with a freight and had turned on the triangle ready for the run back south. She stands in the damp atmosphere waiting for the 'dolly' to come off to allow her to set back into the sidings. Standard '4' 2-6-0s Nos 76035-044 were allocated to Neasden and put in fine performances in their ridiculously short lives. *G. C. Farnell*

Below:

Before the BR Standard 2-6-4Ts arrived, the stylish Thompson 'L1s' were used alongside with LMR Fairburn and Stanier types. Here 'L1' No 67792, complete with headcode disc, runs towards Princes Risborough with a Marylebone service in June 1956. *G. C. Farnell*

Right:
Driver Les Newman and Fireman Keith West are pictured on the platform at Woodford while waiting to relieve the crew of the 17.15 from Nottingham Victoria. Les had recently transferred to Marylebone having spent 20 years on electrics at Watford Junction. Keith was quite a character who in a short railway career served at Leicester Central, Cricklewood, Marylebone and Leicester Midland and finally saw out the final days of steam on the Southern Region at Nine Elms. *Author's Collection*

Below:
Metropolitan electric locomotive No 5 *John Hampden* waits at Amersham for the return of a Metropolitan special from Aylesbury as a four-car DMU leaves for Aylesbury on 26 May 1963. *Brian Stephenson*

Top right:
The 21.10 DMU to Aylesbury waits to leave Platform 3 at Marylebone on 19 January 1966, nine months before through services were withdrawn. *J. Clarke*

Below centre:
Another steam-hauled suburban service approaches Wendover with a Standard '4' 2-6-4T in charge in May 1955. *G. C. Farnell*

Below right:
A Marylebone train climbs towards Amersham from Aylesbury with Fairburn '4MT' 2-6-4T No 42252 in charge in June 1957. These locomotives were excellent machines. *G. C. Farnell*

Above left:
A Fairburn 2-6-4T struggles through Wendover with a goods working from Woodford in the heavy snow of January 1962. *G. C. Farnell*

Left:
A BR Standard '4' 2-6-0 on a pick-up working shunts the yard at Wendover, whilst a Fairburn 2-6-4T departs for Aylesbury in October 1958. *G. C. Farnell*

Above:
Although the GC was by this time almost exclusively worked by LMR motive power, 'V2s' still occasionally appeared; York's No 60954, mysteriously 'borrowed', heads the 16.38 Marylebone-Nottingham semi-fast between Amersham and Great Missenden on 15 June 1963.
Brian Stephenson

Right:
A Stanier '8F' 2-8-0 with a pick-up freight is seen from a DMU having been shunted at Great Missenden to let a semi-fast pass through on the down main line. The permanent way gang in the distance prepare to get out of the way. *G. C. Farnell*

Right:
'N5' Tank No 69341 runs light through Harrow-on-the-Hill for servicing at Neasden. The locomotive worked the Chesham branch and was introduced in 1891 — a Parker MS&L design still looking good in March 1959. *G. C. Farnell*

Below:
With closure now formally announced for through services, 'Black Five' 4-6-0 No 45190 waits to leave Marylebone with the 16.38 semi-fast train for Nottingham on 30 April 1966. *P. H. Groom*

Top:
**Stanier 'Black Five'
No 45454 has just arrived
at Lutterworth with the
08.15 Nottingham
Victoria-Marylebone on
12 March 1966.**
M. Mitchell

Above right:
**'Black Five' No 45292
leaves a quiet Leicester
Central station with the
17.15 Nottingham-
Marylebone on 31 July
1965.** *G. D. King*

Right:
**The last 17.15
Nottingham-Marylebone
service takes water at
Rugby Central with 'Black
Five' No 44984 in charge,
complete with wreath. The
train and its balancing
working, the 22.45
Marylebone-Manchester,
ran to time in both
directions, despite the
unkempt appearance of
the locomotive.**
E. J. S. Gadsden

**The semi-fasts were replaced by a truncated DMU
service from Rugby to Nottingham only. All track was
rationalised and no marketing of the service took place.
On 5 May 1969 it fell to Signalman Albert Fawkes to lock
up Leicester Central station for the last time.**
Leicester Mercury